The Other Universe

'The art of divine Magic consists in the ability to perceive the essence of things in the light of nature, and—by using the soul-powers of the Spirit—to produce material things from the unseen universe, and in such operations the Above and the Below must be brought together and made to act harmoniously.'

The Secret Doctrine. H. P. Blavatsky

JOHN R. SINCLAIR

The Other Universe

RIDER AND COMPANY
LONDON

RIDER AND COMPANY
3 Fitzroy Square, London W1

AN IMPRINT OF THE  HUTCHINSON GROUP

London Melbourne Sydney Auckland
Wellington Johannesburg Cape Town
and agencies throughout the world

First published 1973

This book has been set in Bembo type, printed in Great Britain on antique wove paper by Anchor Press, and bound by Wm. Brendon, both of Tiptree, Essex

ISBN 0 09 113890 6 (cased)
0 09 113891 4 (paper)

Contents

Acknowledgements

Grateful thanks to the following publishing houses for permission to quote from their authors' work: The Oxford University Press, Collins Publishers, Routledge & Kegan Paul, Harcourt Brace Jovanovich, Faber & Faber, The Theosophical Publishing House, the Lucis Press. My thanks also to Mr. C. A. McIntyre for checking the original MSS.

A full list of titles mentioned or quoted in the text is given at the end of the book, with authors' names.

Thanks are due to a great number of good friends who helped and encouraged this work in many ways, both during the journey when the idea for this book came along, as well as before and after. Special thanks are due to Florence, Jeanne, Nancy, Miriam, Suni, Robert, Walter and Roberto who made this part of 'the trip' possible.

Preface

In discussing this subject of magic, how shall we approach each other?

There is an exercise, sometimes used in studios of theatre arts, in which the student uses an ordinary kitchen chair as a basic prop which can become anything. His imagination converts it from motor car to clothes chest. But part of the game, as each one in the group approaches the chair, is not to work out in one's mind beforehand how to make such and such an effect, but rather to surprise oneself, and suddenly find it possible to make the corners of the chair back become hot and cold taps with the seat as hand-basin. Or in handling the chair to discover oneself sheltering beneath an umbrella. Whether you cheat or not is your own business. The fun of the exercise lies in making something alive and vital take place.

Human beings are always improvising. Often, it is true, on a basis of very considerable knowledge and experience. But they are responsible for handling that knowledge to shape the new. Dr. Von Braun, the leader of America's space programme, pointed out in a television interview shown around the time of the first moon landing that man's capacity to deal with the unexpected was the human faculty which machines and computers, however complex, could not duplicate. And certainly many a politician must have escaped lynching by an inspired conversion of programme, policies or even himself!

Magic is largely a business of the conversion of energies, whether one looks at it mystically, metaphysically or materially. And every man is a potential magician. In terms of the light being shed by modern physics on the experiences of living, if not on life itself, every human being is a conjury of energies working with energy in a veritable sea of variously qualified energies.

To many people the subject of magic will simply have rather vague overtones of Fraser's *The Golden Bough*, or even the more lurid phenomena of spiritualism and the occult which may have cropped up in some horror story. I have myself peered into the workings of a variety of esoteric groups, and while I believe the societies and associations who concern themselves with such interests do genuinely hold keys to what might be called the theory and philosophy of magic, there are few actual magicians to be found amongst their membership ranks.

Probably those fledgling magicians the race has so far produced are currently amongst our scientists and business men, with a spattering of mathematicians and artists of one sort of another, the odd psychiatrist, medical or social worker and a number of people who can weave spells wherever they may be situated. However, these are the ones who are on their way and know what they do. Part of this book's purpose is to take a look at what might be called the philosophy of magic, as a way of life, and see if it cannot be applied rather practically by the ordinary citizen in the face of today's problems.

This does not mean making a doctrine out of the whole

thing. To illustrate points, I shall, where it seems appropriate, tell of some of the experiences I have had with esoteric groups. On the surface their beliefs were often widely different. Yet I have found a certain underlying unity between many of them, almost as if they operated as the various faculties and lecture halls of some vast invisible university. Some of the professors obviously had better material than others, but none the less all were held together by a broad common purpose.

For instance, there may at first appear to be small connection between, say, Aldous Huxley's Vedanta-based perennial philosophy and Bernard Shaw's vigorous ideas on creative evolution, yet both in essence and in some of the reaction they evoke a similar impulse becomes evident. It is not merely in a misty mystical flavour that philosophies like these and some of the co-called secret doctrines of masonry, theosophy, new thought, spiritualism, yoga, and so on, have relationship. They are joint heirs of what has been called the ageless wisdom teaching; a synthesising and universal teaching which represents an approach to life belonging to no particular age or place in history, but none the less one which emerges time and again re-dressed to suit the occasion and the scene and in order to jog man out of bigotry and narrow doctrinaire imprisonment.

A vague friend, wishing to be congenial and take an interest in what concerned me, got his adjectives slightly mixed up when he referred to 'this ageless, toothless wisdom you talk of . . .'. Perhaps this present enquiry really relates to the subject of teeth. Does the ageless wisdom of the secret doctrines have enough bite to be practical nowadays, or is it part of a strange fancy to be dusted out of the modern mind like the bric-à-brac of an outdated Victorian drawing room?

And, further, can it affect our individual lives in a practical and creative way? Clearly there have been a few rare creatures in history whose lives have been magical in some way or another. But what about the rest of us who are not exceptions, and who normally bumble along with our weaknesses and our confusions? To what degree can we be caught up in the broad sweep of creative evolution? Can that which is magical play a part in our own smallish orbit? And through us, each in his own place, can there be any sort of transfiguration from the grass roots of human society?

The very words magic and magus take their roots from a similar source as such words as magnificent and magnanimous. As Bernard Shaw implies in his epic drama cycle *Back to Methuselah*, the quest is glory. And the same point is made in world religions, witness Christ's prayer in Chapter 17 of St. John's Gospel. We are asking what, in our day, can we do to behold the glory of life, and incidentally the glory of man, as one of life's vehicles?

I *Revolt in Heaven*

KING AND BARONS

A short while ago I visited the Suffolk town of Bury St. Edmunds. Going round the ruins of the old abbey centre I suddenly met up with a quaint bit of early nineteenth-century verse, engraved on a tablet in one of the crumbling flintstone pillars.

> Where the rude buttress totters to its fall
> And ivy mantles o'er the crumbling wall;
> Where e'en the skilful eye can scarcely trace
> The once High Altar's lowly resting place—
> Let patriotic fancy muse awhile
> Amid the ruins of this ancient pile,
> Six weary centuries have past away;
> Palace and Abbey moulder in decay—
> Cold death enshrouds the learned and the brave
> Langton—FitzWalter—slumber in the grave,
> But still we read in deathless records, how
> The high-soul'd priest confirmed the Baron's vow:
> And Freedom, unforgetful, still recites
> This second birth-place of our native Rights.

The pillar holding up this reminder of preparatory work done prior to the barons' historic confrontation of

King John at Runnymede stood near to where the high altar of the one-time abbey must have been. Alongside this place a huge copper beech spread out its branches. The remains of the cloisters where the monks once walked were planted gardens with lilac and laburnum trees. And further on, towards the new abbey, stood a rose terrace donated by an American visitor of wartime days.

It was in this location that twenty-five representatives, carefully listed on another tablet, of the English barons met to discuss the Magna Carta. Here they debated tactics and vision under the chairmanship of Cardinal Stephen Langton, and together dedicated themselves before the high altar to the successful consummation of that vision.

It is part of modern training in positive thinking to consider life's problems as opportunities and challenges. Unfortunately, this perspective on things is sometimes delayed beyond the point where the challenge is within manageable proportions. Add to this the fact that the contemporary scene comprises a tangled mass of problem challenges, and one finds individuals sinking back into the understandable viewpoint that problems are a rotten old swamp out of which one's got to try and splash as best one may.

However, it is possible even within the limitations of any given situation to take some degree of initiative and challenge life in the same way as the barons challenged King John with their new vision. We do not have to remain passive until some overweight problem, private or communal, throws down its gauntlet before us.

Do not accept my word for this. The suggestion of another person, while it may have value, is still secondhand. Observe for yourself and see if you cannot spot the continual challenge and counter-challenge that is going on between life and consciousness.

Life is a bit like King John representing the domain, the *status quo*, a given set of circumstances, the scene as it is, and containing both restriction and opportunity; possibly a drain on one's resources but also a fount of treasure. Consciousness is, in turn, represented by the barons; no doubt initially split up amongst themselves, fragmented and pulled apart by different interests, but coming together as one almighty vision grows amongst them. In their midst, the figure of the Cardinal playing the part of wise councillor, guiding conscience, a link with some hidden source of inspiration. And the meeting of the two, life and consciousness, King and barons, making Magna Carta a fact, anchoring something creative for men to live with.

Watching this interplay one is bound to ask if it is necessary for the meeting of consciousness with life to take place in the atmosphere of sniping warfare that so often prevails. As far as the human race is concerned they are interdependent. Of course, friction can be valuable in promoting growth, but carried beyond a certain point it can also burn up what it may originally have awoken from dense inertia. So must consciousness always and inevitably wrestle with life, like the barons did with John, before a major advance is made? Sometimes it would seem so. Even religious teaching talks of 'taking the Kingdom of Heaven by storm', and men have used scripture to promote some of the most devastating conflicts of all time. And yet some of the greatest souls the world has produced have hinted that there is another way which men can adopt when a certain measure of maturity is reached, the kernel of this other way being the fact that life contains the seed or essence of a creative destiny with which it is possible for man and men to co-operate consciously.

CERTAIN ESOTERIC SCHOOLS

One group of esoteric schools with which I have been acquainted geared much of their work towards training students to be sensitive to what they regarded as a divine plan for enlightenment and loving understanding. Of course, this has been the broad objective of many religious groups, but in thinking about magic it will be interesting to describe roughly how the schools went about their work. Their activity and goals will illustrate at least one sort of technical and deliberate preparation for the mystical marriage of life and consciousness.

The schools themselves originated as so many pioneering enterprises tend to do, in the self-initiated efforts of a small group of individuals led in the main by one teacher.

Their initial work in putting the ageless wisdom teachings before the public through writings, lectures and personal contact gained recognition and response. In order to cope with the interest, what had started as a circular distributed between a few students snowballed until it became an organised school. Eventually this parent school spread its influence into most countries where totalitarian influences do not stifle free research. And in due season it seeded as former students started other training programmes and allied projects.

These schools, in common with other genuinely esoteric groups, do not deliberately advertise their presence. There are, of course, a number of organisations who make no pretence of being esoteric schools who promote some feature of the ageless wisdom and quite naturally make use of public information media. The work of the schools being rather hard, they tend to cater for an individual here and there. And such people find their way to the schools or other training groups by enquiry. They meet someone, they read a book, a chance word in a conversation or some other form of contact puts them in touch.

This is as well, because in this particular group of schools there is really little to carry the student who has not got it in him to be self-taught. Teaching is there, a certain degree of guidance is there, but the only real exams are the ones the student devises for himself. And there is no one who has much time to apply either crook or flail.

Training groups do exist, of course, where there is a certain amount of personal contact with someone acting as instructor, and where students work in company on activities designed to awaken consciousness. However, in the particular schools of which I am now writing the work is mostly sent to the student through the post. Reports and papers are requested in the majority of cases so that a check can be kept, and also to give the student some practice in grounding concepts which might otherwise drift by his vision. It matters very little who tells us what, the subject matter is unhelpful in extremity and crisis unless we have in some way been able to make it our own. And even an intellectual understanding expressed in writing can be some sort of first step towards proper digestion.

A familiar procedure with those schools in the group running regular courses of study is for students to be allotted to a corresponding secretary who comments on their work. In some instances it would take a little while for a student to lose the familiar children's-school feeling that they were working to please teacher. But the penny would drop, usually sooner than later, that they really were their own instructor, working with that which was already in them. And there is in fact a neat story of the founder of the original school remarking that it was encouraging how many students got on in spite of their secretaries!

To keep this working relationship impersonal the student is very frequently in a different country to the secretary. However, as nearly everyone travels about so much nowadays this is not the foil it was a few decades ago. But then there is also no doubt less likelihood of people falling foul of the personality cult than there used to be. Modern society has been disabused of so many illusions.

The secretaries are unpaid for their services and in fact as far as I know all the schools in the group run on a voluntary donation basis. This provision allows participation by people in countries where currency restrictions are in force, even though a school may have no office or agent there. It is also designed to awaken the student's own sense of gratitude and responsibility for promoting the work, once he satisfies himself that the teachings are helpful.

FINANCIAL SUPPLY

An understanding of money as yet another kind of energy over which we have some degree of trusteeship may only grow gradually. So much emotion is tied in to this means of subsistence. We have to work with whatever we have in hand at the moment. Metaphysicians are right in stressing that the doorways of supply are opened by starting to give. One may not have cash in hand at any given moment, but there may be something in the house, lying static in a cupboard, that we can put into circulation. One dear suburban lady said she wished she had some diamonds, then she would be able to sell them for the sake of the work! But that, of course, is not the point, we cannot contribute what we wish we had, only what we've got. And that is not such a statement of the obvious as it appears, if one just stops to examine the fantasies we all indulge in with relation to money.

Another area where clarification can take time is in relation to what we give to. This is especially true of giving for altruistic, educational or insubstantial purposes. Down-to-earth concrete demands of family or community are fairly obvious, and we decide what to give to what according to our inclinations and pledged commitments. But with something impersonal that may show no immediate material return our attitude is inclined to be a good deal more uncertain. Here a considerable strength of personal conviction is a necessary trigger.

Nowadays there is a great deal of emphasis on what might be called creative giving. That is, there is a growth in understanding that money is a life-giving energy which, rightly handled, can help something underdeveloped to stand on its own feet and vitalise its own subsistence centres. This is obviously a healthy move from former ideas about the dutiful hand-outs, which are so often swallowed whole without healing the condition that made the need for them.

These things may seem to be a far cry from the magic we set out to discuss. But when we talk about magic being the conversion of energy it's not hard to see that the energies we handle every day are the ones we must start with. And money is surely concretised energy. In any event, behind all giving lies an attitude of heart and mind. It takes the blending of these two—warmth to empower the giving hand, and discretion to place the seed.

Emotional response leading to a release of material provision, is usually widespread when mass disaster or tragedy appeal. Beyond this, the more thoughtful recognise that feeling needs to be educated by reason and foresight, as well as the sudden call of dire need. But there is also a faculty called the straight-knowledge of the heart, an intuitional penetration that transcends reason and feeling and yet is compounded of them both. This can act swiftly and without any rigidity, and often discovers a real need where it may not be obvious.

There is a famous report about Mme Blavatsky, authoress of *The Secret Doctrine*, who had just embarked on board ship on a journey from Europe to America. Standing on deck looking over the rail, she became aware of a young mother and child in distress on the quay. She discovered they had to get to America, but had not got enough for the passage. Immediately, so the report goes, she cashed in her first-class ticket, sponsored the woman who had impressed her in some way and went steerage with her and her infant.

Once, I remember meeting a rather bedraggled woman with a small child, who asked me for some money in the street. Familiar with importunate beggars who canvas a street corner as though it were a business pitch, whom it is rash to encourage with hand-outs, I went on towards an appointment. Something held me up and I turned round and gave the woman, who had also gone on her way, a much smaller coin than the amount she asked and I handed the child a not very interesting sweet that happened to be in my pocket. Then they went on. As they disappeared I knew that in that precise situation, not some other generalised one, I had not done what was necessary. It wasn't particularly the couple's faces that one recalls, the woman's brutalised and bloated and the child's white and stony. It was their backs. Their backs disappearing in a darkening, wind-swept street taking yet another tiny, personal, disguised and missed opportunity with them.

THREE-POINTED CURRICULUM

The programme of work devised and used by the group of esoteric schools I set out to discuss is based on three factors: meditation to awaken consciousness to that which is transcendental, study to embellish the mind content and service to ground the whole enterprise in practice.

Service is an old-styled word now. But it is undoubtedly a means of making that other overworked word 'love' into a tangible commodity. In terms of human growth and maturity service is a science. That may take the glamour out of it for some, but think of it this way: To go into some form of service puts one on the spot. It makes demands on one's resources. It tests out one's theories. It provokes one to think what one is really doing. The more clear one's motive and the more self-initiated the service, the more this is true. If you happen to be trying out some sort of service project, and a lot of people are without perhaps using that exact word, just take a look at the operation and see if this is not so.

By service, we mean, in this context, something that really is of benefit. It might involve one's employment or the provision of goods, but the attitude behind the activity will be one of goodwill.

In direct relation to the schools, service is in the main left to the individual. Each person having a different environment and varied resources, it is necessarily a private decision. The school merely points out the desirability of finding a practical outlet for aspiration. And also indicates that some people discover, in the course of self-study, that they have a soul-vocation, something which is in them to contribute to the world in terms of talent, service or vision, which, once they start coming into their own in a spiritual sense, is not to be blocked by circumstance.

As time went by, certain projects were evolved by some of the schools, particularly in the case of the parent school within the group. And individual students are invited to contribute to these services if they wish. However, they are in the main confined to the most subjective forms of public work such as the service of invocation and prayer for the general good and the production of educational literature. On the whole, as no dangerous techniques requiring immediate supervision are involved, the policy of encouraging and coaxing the self-taught student seems to work best.

Some people feel the advice given by the old general to the young officer to 'Keep away from headquarters, they're dangerous places', is applicable in relation to the organisational centres of these schools. However, I would think that while there is a natural tendency to theorise in any administrative office, and much of the vital response to real need which justifies the schools' existence takes place in the field, yet the devoted routine work in the various school offices does keep the whole show on the road.

The study aspect of the schools acquaints the student with the general background of the ageless wisdom-teaching, highlights certain principles and suggests certain reading on the subject of the hidden aspects of man's constitution. An eager and questing mind would take all this in its stride, sorting out what seems immediately applicable and letting the rest ride by for the time being. But certain types of more rigid minds whose content is already set or relatively underdeveloped tend to suffer a bit from mental indigestion. Although streamlined and edited in the course of development by the various different schools in the group, the study material contains a good deal more than the average member of the public is accustomed to work on outside college life, though business and professional people could take it in their stride if they were keen.

A good deal of all this material, as we have indicated, consists of an occultist's viewpoint of the constitution of man. What man is, both in form and essence, and in terms of potential possibilities. And one's absorption of the information really depends on the vitality of one's interest.

These two aspects of practical work and theoretical study are balanced and united by active meditation work. This is reported on regularly, as it would be easy enough for students to get lost in the highways and byways of subjectivity. Most schools of meditation which I have come across in the Western world adopt some form of surveillance on their students, at least in the early stages of work. Actually, as there are now so many schools, each usually meaning something slightly different by the word 'meditation', a little further investigation into it will do no harm.

MEDITATION AND THE ANTAHKARANA

Meditation is a natural faculty of human consciousness. It is the method consciousness adopts in order to relate to life in a meaningful way, and it is because of this that I have started off by discussing these esoteric schools at some length. We all meditate. We ponder, we research, we observe, we consider, we identify and reflect; the words of explanation are endless. What various groups usually mean when they say they teach meditation is that they give instruction in a technique or an approach which, in their opinion, will boost an individual's meditative capacity.

When I had the interesting experience of visiting N.A.S.A., the American space-project base near Houston, Texas, I was intrigued to learn the name of the tower structure placed alongside the mighty rockets designed for space travel. No doubt this name had been mentioned in literature and film, but I had not taken in its significance until that moment. Because of its function in fuelling, feeding and cradling the rocket prior to take-off it is referred to as the umbilical tower.

The purpose of a meditation technique, so-called, is somewhat similar: a certain pattern, a mental ritual or exercise is designed to help a lift-off in consciousness.

The important thing is that it is the rocket that takes off, not the umbilical tower. One should not get trapped by any form of meditation, and this will not occur if one understands its uses.

The form or ritual of meditation employed by our group of schools is that which ancient instructions in raja yoga, often termed the kingly science of the mind, call 'meditation upon a seed'. A seed concept or idea, often clothed in a passage of scripture, an affirmation or similar statement, is taken as a subject for the mind to give its attention to. This seed-thought then acts on the currents of mental activity rather like a magnet.

Most people will recall the demonstration in junior science classes where a magnet is placed under a sheet of paper on which some iron filings have been sprinkled. The iron filings then fall into order according to the current of the magnet's force-field. Something similar occurs in the use of a seed-thought. And it is possible to gain some appreciation of our own mental content during this experiment, as our sundry mental iron filings squiggle around and line themselves up in relation to the force field generated around a particular seed-thought.

The esoteric schools we have mentioned, along with many others, believe in man's capacity for bridging the gap between the familiar everyday area of reactive mental, emotional and physical energy and an inspiring, essential realm of energy, for which the first are intended as reflectors or relays. The transcendental realm is looked on as the indivisible triune spheres hinted at in many world religions. The quotation with which we have prefaced this book calls it 'the unseen universe'. The term often used for the bridge between the two realms is a double word of Sanskrit origin, antahkarana. This has been translated as meaning 'inner instrument'. And we may reasonably take it that in the intuitive and creative sensitivity of a mature human being we have the representation of this inner instrument. It is not the prerogative of any group or system, it is certainly not provided by any school, but is very simply the effort of life and consciousness to come to terms constructively at as many levels as possible.

The value of the work done by these esoteric schools lies in its highlighting of the existence of the antahkarana, and also in pointing out that although mankind has far to go in its development, the purpose of this inner instrument is to increase man's creativity through synthesising all his energies and resources.

INTERNAL REVOLUTION

Though having said this, one has to appreciate immediately that we are really in no position to say what all man's energies are. Very often, in the short run, a rather narrow, selfish, one-pointed activity may seem to achieve more than one which submits individual effort to a larger picture. Waking all the deep-laid energies of man's being, even in so far as we know them, may initially cause considerable upheaval in the *status quo*. What seems like a simple step of widening our horizon can cause and require a thorough-going internal revolution.

What goes on within an individual human being in terms of his embryo inner instrument can affect him psychologically and also physiologically. And through the quality of the radiation and discharge of his own particular energy field it can affect his environment, without his necessarily having taken deliberate outward action.

One of the technical routes whereby subjective activity becomes objective is the network of subtle electrical energy centres lying back behind the endocrine glandular system and certain nerve plexii of the human body. Eastern teaching on the 'chakras', as they have been called, is now generally familiar to most people who have studied some facet of the ageless wisdom-teaching, at least as a theory or working hypothesis. A recent book by Dr. Shafica Karagulla, M.D., called *Breakthrough to Creativity* discusses these centres in layman's language as part of a research experiment. In a chapter on 'Energy Fields and Medical Diagnosis' she reports, for example, the compared observations of clairvoyants who had examined the state of a subject's energy centres in relation to regular diagnosis made by a medical specialist.

Dr. Karagulla's book simply presents some of the observations to date of a research foundation with which she is connected. A term she makes use of in describing some of the additional types of sensitivity displayed by certain gifted people is 'higher sense perception'. This phrase could also describe one sort of endowment relating to our antahkarana or inner instrument.

To return to my remark about an inner revolution it is intriguing that several psychiatrists have recently made use of the term 'a Copernican revolution' to describe a particular psychological development. Copernicus, as you know, pointed out a fact, subsequently confirmed by Galileo, that the earth revolved round the sun and not the other way round. This was a rude shock to the egocentric establishment of the day, who felt man to be the supreme creature at the centre of the universe. However, once the seemingly bitter pill was swallowed and digested it gave a new sense of proportion and a more realistic understanding of the nature of things. An inner psychological revolution which brings us new insight in the way Copernicus brought light to his era helps to decentralise the tight vortex of human egotism and dispel the fog of illusion.

Each one of us goes through many such revolutions in the course of development. There is the day in our childhood it dawns upon us that perhaps our parents do have other interests beside ourselves, or when we discover that maybe the boy-friend or girl-friend of adolescence just occasionally does have another date! Each one of us can find similar awakening shocks, which once absorbed make for maturity. On the other hand, if we deny these inner revolutions we move on towards rigidity of ego.

After a time, as we become more skilful in the ways of the world, it is easier to turn aside the discomforting effects of the personal Copernican revolution. We learn how to dodge it. But in doing so we forgo a peculiar opportunity for growth, and perhaps thereby contribute to the ageing effect of psychological crystallisation. The alternative is to understand the Copernican revolution for what it is, and, by welcoming it, use its force constructively, rather as a ju-jutsu expert may give way in order to employ the force of an opponent. What it amounts to, does it not? is that in order to remain sensitive we must remain open. This openness involves vulnerability, but also promises growth.

In a paper, *The Training of the Will*, published by the Psychosynthesis Research Foundation of New York, the President, an Italian psychiatrist, Dr. Roberto Assagioli,

M.D., writes about this. Under the heading 'The Relation of our Will to the Universal Will—Recognition of Our True Place in the Universe', he says:

> It can be achieved easily by means of an exercise of reflective meditation. Let us subdue the activity of our mind, quiet our emotions, 'make silence' in ourselves—at least to some extent. Then let the sense of the infinite grandeur of the universe permeate us; let us feel ourselves to be a small particle in it, similar to myriads of other particles; let us realise that we are one of many millions of inhabitants of a small globe—one of the planets of a star which is in its turn only one of billions of suns forming a galaxy, and that the galaxies are countless. Such a meditation produces, little by little, or sometimes instantaneously, an inner change that might be called an inner 'Copernican revolution'. We no longer live and act as if we were at the centre of the universe: the true proportions and relations between it and ourselves are established. Yet, by a curious psychological paradox, instead of feeling small and humiliated, we experience a sense of expansion, a new dignity. We lose our false sense of importance, the pompousness of our pride and the conceit about our personal merits; we feel ourselves in tune with the universe; even more we feel that we are made of its substance, as a drop of water is made of the same substance of the ocean. We recognise ourselves to be an integral part of it and feel the joy of this recognition.
>
> From this meditation we return to our everyday life more poised and serene and also with a clearer insight into personal and practical problems. The remembrance of it will remain to support us through trying and painful times. . . .

If we are to understand this whole business of the Copernican revolution in connection with life and consciousness we have to observe very acutely what happens to us in relation to conditioning and freedom. Our consciousness, our outlook, is subject to conditioning all the time, is it not? Social background, national prejudices, religious upbringing, educational training, all play their part, do they not? Only as there is some fundamental shift in attitude does new life burst through consciousness and bring a measure of freedom. But almost immediately the conditioning starts again, albeit from a new direction. And before long the crystallisation of thinking around some new set of ideas is as hard-set as the previous pattern. So a full and final Copernican revolution cannot ever be behind us. If we consent to growth we are always in the midst of it.

And what works in relation to the individual is also true for the multitude of individuals who make up society. This is markedly visible at our present point in history when so many social and geographical boundaries are being altered and civilisation is under the impact of energies which force major reappraisal.

The poet Christopher Fry, taking an optimistic outlook in his play *A Sleep of Prisoners*, used the imagery of an ice-floe subject to the spring thaw. He saw the possibility of centuries of frozen human misery being melted.

> The human heart can go to the lengths of God.
> Dark and cold we may be, but this
> Is no winter now. The frozen misery
> Of centuries breaks, cracks, begins to move;
> The thunder is the thunder of the flows,
> The thaw, the flood, the upstart Spring.
> Thank God our time is now when wrong
> Comes up to face us everywhere,
> Never to leave us till we take
> The longest stride of soul men ever took.
> Affairs are now soul size.
> The enterprise
> Is exploration into God,
> Where no nation's foot has ever trodden yet.

Where are you making for? It takes
So many thousand years to wake,
But will you wake—for pity's sake?

This mind's-eye picture is a helpful vision. Poets can often clarify an issue without getting involved in any partisan approach. However, if we are prepared to look at the picture, and then care to reflect on its implications, we will realise that an ice-pack at break-up point can be a dangerous thing. The isolated icebergs freed from the mass to which they belonged clash and strain together. The tensions of national and international society are not dissimilar. Only a further melting, and consequent reduction to their pure state, can ease the tension of the ice-floe. This melting has to take place in consciousness, where attitude can affect action.

THE POLAR OPPOSITES

Now, abandoning the poet's vision and looking directly at the world around us, there is one item, which we will find is vitally connected with the practice of magic, which dominates our human problems. It does not matter what our particular interest on the social scene may be. Whether we have taken up cudgels in the area of racial disturbance, labour relations or economics, or whether we try to discover unity among the churches, a just deal in education or the fulfilment of any other personal or collective hope, we find ourselves involved in the struggle of dualities. It is quite natural that we should. We live in a dualistic system.

Light and dark, hot and cold, these natural differences are obvious and we accept them. But then nature manages her duality much better than man does. With man, duality becomes infinitely subtle. We find system against system, plan against plan, and for every idea proposed, whether good or not so good, there is another to oppose it. And while we continue to dream about heaven we end up by materialising hell.

Given our innate violence, the formulation of any centre of energy, whether it is a family or an organisation or the establishment of the individual in a chosen environment, is an invitation to conflict. The automatic reflexes of pull and repulsion make this so. Look around, observe and see if this isn't so at some level, psychological or emotional, if not actually physical. This occurs again and again, however worthy and however idealistic the centre or unit of energy may be.

Let us look at duality in terms of magic. Without going into any involved kabalistic terminology, let us consider some of the essential differences between so-called white magic and black magic, and see if we cannot find a clue to the understanding of our dualistic system while considering these ancient opponents.

WHITE MAGIC AND BLACK

Old myths speak of a time when men, aware of the knowledge of good and evil, divided amongst themselves and chose to work with the evolution of nature or against it. Whether such myths are considered as having a basis in factual history or not is irrelevant to our main theme. They illustrate a happening within the unfolding evolution of human consciousness. And in this respect myths often give a much more unbiased account of what is really going on than the surface events of partisan history.

In stories of the fabled Atlantean civilisation this schism is reported as becoming a prominent influence in human affairs. Picturesque names describe the two factions. Those who sought to trap nature's energies for selfish and therefore limited aggrandisement were referred to as the Lords of Dark Countenance, while the ones who were prepared to work with the universal storehouse in a co-operative way for the general weal were known as the Lords of the Shining Face. The implication being that they reflected the light of the central spiritual sun.

Much of their magic was the science of the day. And in so far as this was the case the techniques of both parties, as distinct from method of application, would be largely the same. The crucial difference lay in motive. And exactly the same distinction applies today. In fact in our time it carries more force because of the mental growth and development of masses of people, and their consequent ability to recognise motive clearly.

In so far as the would-be magician must operate through our dualistic environment, the really nitty-gritty question must examine his relationship to that duality. Does he exploit it to his selfish advantage? Does he inflame the dualistic condition so that opposites become ever more explosive sources of conflict? Does he ride to power on the emotive waves of bigotry, ignorant prejudice and separationism? Or is he prepared to endure what often turns out to be the considerable agony of the middle point, mediating, co-ordinating, and reconciling? In other words, working in so far as he possibly can above duality, at a point of synthesis that visions healthy polar opposites not as opponents but as co-operative potencies for creativity.

The very names black and white magic, with the automatic emotional and psychological response we have to these colours, are indicative of our dualistic nature. Later on we may attempt a more accurate naming. For the moment let us fall back on the accustomed names until we can jump free of them.

We started this work with a mention of Shaw's ideas of Lamarckian creative evolution. And even if this particular philosophy is not our own precise way of looking at things it gives an indication of life and consciousness in creative union and advance. This concept we can translate for ourselves as we will. The frame of reference is less important than that the concept be alive. Now, if white magic is the agent of this evolutionary trend, then black magic as its polar opposite will be concerned with the contrary trend of involution or the laying down of the raw material of chaos from which ordered beauty must eventually be lifted.

And although one can sense the balancing nature of the two within the larger scheme of things, one should beware of compromise at our level of present awareness. Although the real black magicians, in contradistinction to the unwise sensation-seeker, are sometimes referred to as our Brothers of the Shadow, they are in fact anti-man. Their usefulness to human evolution is that of the decomposing corpse which can enrich the earth, but which if left to rot in the open, spreads a pestilence.

In representing these two streams of activity, the magicians are sometimes named the brothers of the right- and left-hand paths. The symbol for both is the five-pointed star. This is also called the pentagram or endless knot, in that the line goes from point to point without break. The right-hand way is represented by the ascendant star, like Leonardo's famous diagram of the proportions of man with arms and legs extended in radiation and head erect. The left-hand way is marked by the falling star, the lone point plunging to earth.

These symbols are not idly chosen. They are indicative of the flow of energy circulating through the vitality centres of the one who works in magic. Both employ the chakras of hands and feet, the implements of human work and mobility. The dark way thereafter relies on the degeneration of the creative function and the degradation of material force as a means of seduction. In order to enslave the dark system must project every sort of illusion.

Where the worker in light is concerned the emphasis is on the lead given through the centres in the upper half of the body, using dedicated speech as the means of communication.* We will go into the significance of sound and words as an instrument of magic later on.

The dark-countenanced manipulator, like a miser counting gold for its own sake, sets to work directly on the many aspects of substantial matter. The enlightened one, in the manner of a just trustee, only approaches matter through the agency of a unifying purpose for which it is to be employed.

If one ponders the legend of the hero Perseus and his meeting with the Gorgon Medusa, one can see this pictorially displayed. The Medusa's countenance, surmounted by writhing serpents, is like the many seemingly independent forces in matter whose chaotic nature can turn a man to stone. Perseus, as you will remember, never

*The function of all the vitality centres has been discussed elsewhere. See *The Mystical Ladder*, Chapter I.

looked the Gorgon directly in the face, but turning his back on her he used his shield as a reflector. He decapitated the monster, by recognising it as a shadow which could not hypnotise.

The reflecting shield is like the enlightened motivation of the worker in the right-sand stream. In many pictures of either Perseus or Pallas Athene, his patroness, the Gorgon's severed head is pictured at the centre of the shield or slung round the neck, by the throat chakra. This is emblematic of the purposeful uniting of the many forces of matter in terms of creative usefulness. The same significance is to be found in the single serpent of wisdom on the head-dress of the initiated Pharaohs, showing that the many serpents of chaos have been brought together and directed.

By and large we can say therefore that black magic is concerned with the form of things. In other words, it manipulates shells. White magic occupies itself with the essential life or spirit within any form. For this reason the selfish worker may often have a quicker apparent success, because the effect of what he does is more immediately visible, whereas the influence of the inner life which has been vivified and stimulated by unselfish, loving work frequently takes a certain time to burst into manifestation. This is very clearly seen in different methods of education. The poet Browning popularised the descriptive phrase 'the imprisoned splendour'.

THE SECRET TEACHING

In a lengthy work, *The Secret Doctrine*, a definition of magic was given by a reputed magician at the end of the last century.

> The art of divine magic consists in the ability to perceive the essence of things in the light of nature, and—by using the soul-powers of the Spirit—to produce material things from the unseen universe, and in such operations the above and the below must be brought together and made to act harmoniously.

The harmony of the above and the below is often symbolised by another star made of two interlaced triangles, the triad of spirit joined with the trinity of manifestation. Thus the six-pointed star of creation. In the book *Isis Unveiled*, by H. P. Blavatsky, who wrote *The Secret Doctrine*, we find the statement: 'The trinity of nature is the lock of magic, the trinity of man the key that fits it.'

The vertical unity of the above and the below or the inner and the outer, which the six-pointed star depicts, indicates the way in which the horizontal duality in the world around us can be surmounted.

Beyond the mental level the human black magician cannot exist. For anything that confines itself to the manipulation of forms, whether those forms be made of mental, emotional or physical matter, cannot penetrate what the ageless wisdom calls the formless worlds.

Because of the limitations of our present vision we are not used to thinking of mental energy in terms of form. But such it is, even though it operates at an extraordinarily rarefied frequency and needs the clothing of denser emotional and physical forms to manifest fully in our eyes. After all, one does hear people talk of thought-forms and the substantiality of ideas.

So long as there is concentration on any form for its own sake, there is conflict. And with form goes duality. Even if that form is just a thought. We know only too well from our own experience in this day and age that ideas can divide men more effectively than any physical wall. In fact the concrete physical wall is only effective if it is policed by those operating at the command of opposing ideas.

Then where is love? Where is the possibility of bringing conflict and friction to a close? Can we really modify the action of duality from a point of synthesis? Is there something beyond the trap of the time and space which provides form with habitation, which, while it is utterly different, can nevertheless transform time and space by the magic of its nature? Is it possible to register with the inner instrument the transcendental unseen universe of *The Secret Doctrine*?

God, the unknown, is often credited with omnipotence. And if, in pure essential energy, in that which is transcendental, we have omnipotence, then by the very nature of the description there is one power, not two. Duality is transcended, because it is not. And it is through the inspiration of that unitary area, without time or space or form as we understand it, that the white magician must learn to work.

When the clatter of turbulent concretisations, swirling emotions and the monkey manipulations of the mind are still, then the unseen universe can communicate. This stillness cannot be induced, it cannot be claimed, it comes in a moment when we think not. There is a synthesis of life and consciousness and creativity ensues.

Perhaps one of the most valuable recent books which helps us to ask ourselves some important Copernican-style questions is J. Krishnamurti's *Freedom from the Known*. The title itself seems indicative of the book's purpose.

THE FORMULA OF RENUNCIATION

Real magic, and there is only one sort, for all else is manipulation and egotism, consists in bringing heaven to earth. It is here on earth that heaven can manifest. And the revolt of the dualities persists while we fail to recognise the other, unseen universe, which is our silent partner.

Paradoxically—and much in magic seems paradoxical—we take steps to end revolt with the acceptance of Copernican revolution in ourselves.

One of the most widely read folk stories of our time is *The Lord of the Rings* by J. R. R. Tolkien. The innocency of this beautifully amalgamated tale has allowed it to be a sort of magic mirror for many people. The author has denied any special symbolic meaning, but it has sparked off interpretative reverie in many people. To my mind, it is interesting that the ring of evil power which had to be unmade was carried back to source by the hobbits, gentle creatures whose simple goodwill made them unambitious. They were supported by the other creatures of Tolkien's Middle-Earth, dwarf and elf and man and aided by the wisdom-master Gandalf. But none of these allies would take the ring for fear of that which was akin to it in their own nature being strengthened to a point where they were overpowered.

Recognition of one power beyond duality means we must appreciate the significance of the Biblical saying: 'Call no man good, for there is but one good—the Father in Heaven.' I think it must be impossible to write of the strange melting of heart, the simple admission of our powerlessness, that allows an entirely unpossessive omnipotence to touch our world.

One of the great of soul who recently visited this world has attempted a hint. It is only a hint because each one has to work out his own revolution. In his *Hymn of the Universe* Teilhard de Chardin gives us what he calls the formula for renunciation:

> The formula of renunciation, if it is to be total, must satisfy two conditions.
>
> It must enable us to go beyond everything there is in the world.
>
> And yet at the same time compel us to press forward (with conviction and passion) the development of this same world.
>
> Speaking in general, Christ gives himself to us through the world which is to be consummated in relation to Him.

2 *The Sorcerer's Apprentice*

THE USE OF RITUAL

One's old friend the *Oxford Pocket Dictionary* says that philosophy is 'the pursuit of wisdom or of the knowledge of things and their causes'. Our attempt to get at the meaning and philosophy and the *raison d'être* for magic in modern times may seem to be a long way from the fairy-tale images of the magician's pointed hat and wand, with which fable has acquainted us. Such things are symbols, outward signs with inward meanings. And it is of more importance that each of us develop his or her own ability to read the symbols that life brings to our individual door than that these pages go into great detail, much of which might be second-hand supposition, anyway, about how to set up a pentagram or cast a spell!

For those that want it these pages do contain a modicum of basic and very practical information, which is safe and helpful. For others this essay may seem to be as elusive as a mystical will o' the wisp. But if it sets them pondering it will still be useful. In any event, let us look at the question of props and aids to magic, and of magical ritual generally.

Ritual is rather like the umbilical tower we spoke of in relation to meditation. It is a framework or a scaffolding. As such it may need highly scientific and precise attention. We know this is true of a rocket-launching. The occasion of the tragedy when three American astronauts were burned in their space craft before it left the ground led to an exhaustive official enquiry which it is said revealed that subcontractors concerned with the preparation of all sorts of equipment had neglected over one hundred points of detail.

The same is true of more insubstantial operations. Take, for example, the production of an opera whose main appeal is the performance of a beautiful and appealing sound. Dance and drama all involve an amalgam of specialist talents and skills. Sir Tyrone Guthrie, the renowned theatrical producer, once gave a television broadcast in which he considered the theatre as ritual, and then looked at that ritual as a means of relating man to his gods, whether they were 'gods' of rustic humour, Aphrodite or the exalted concepts of death and resurrection that the original dramatic rituals of the Dionysian mysteries sought to convey. In this sense he saw actors somewhat as Appolonian priests or mediums.

Shakespeare in *A Midsummer Night's Dream* wrote lines which say something similar to the definition of magic which we took from *The Secret Doctrine*.

> The poet's eye, in a fine frenzy rolling,
> Doth glance from Heaven to Earth, from Earth to Heaven,
> And as imagination bodies forth
> The forms of things unknown, the poet's pen
> Turns them to shapes and gives to airy nothing
> A local habitation and a name.

Guthrie in his talk also put forward the stimulating idea that ritual is an expression of belief in a plan. In terms of *The Secret Doctrine* it is an attempt to trace 'below' a pattern impressed from 'above'. In other words, an attempt to help man's consciousness understand things about life and death not immediately discernible through the senses.

Old mystery rituals find a modern counterpart in the masonic movement. A church service of any sort is designed as a ritual vehicle for certain aspirations and essences of worship and blessing. Nations capsulate their most poignant moments of history in ritual. And so, as it develops from objective scientific procedure through the intangibles of art and aspiration, we can appreciate that ritual has some usefulness in linking us with that which is transcendental.

Not so long ago Laurens van der Post, the well-known writer, took part in a television broadcast which examined religious mystery and mysticism. He commented that besides being an attempt to make life meaningful and to answer doubts and fears about existence, religion could help us become aware of our private and personal contract with life. And following on that it could assist us in obedience to that contract. In this sense ritual is a bit like a form of contract, approved by our particular trade union of belief, on which we base our own agreement to co-operate with what we understand of life's plan.

Like all forms of contract, ritual can therefore be helpful in regulating our work, but it can on occasions also be a bit of a prison, if we don't watch out. Like a contract from which we would rather be released.

Walt Whitman knew this well when he wrote:

> Hurrah for positive science! Long live exact demonstration!
> Your facts are useful, and yet they are not my dwelling,
> I but enter by them to an area of my dwelling.

Ritual also happily has its comical side. Some people will burst into ritual at the slightest provocation. Oh, the rituals of the social welcome! I remember once going to stay with an enchanting lady whom I had not previously met. When I arrived she mentioned that she and her husband just happened to be having a small group of people in that evening and would I speak to them for a short period. As 'that evening' was already on us, I went quickly to my room with about half an hour to pull some thoughts together. When I emerged the downstairs rooms were shrouded with window-shutters. An altar had been set up and decorated with evergreens and naked flame, which did its best to consume the evergreens. Several people were in robes. I must admit that my first reaction was to cast a wary eye around for a sacrificial block—just supposing my talk proved to be an insufficient offering!

One revered European occultist reportedly had very short sight and liked to make use of some kind of eyeglass held in the hand. But as it is more or less impractical to wield a double-handled ritual sword and lorgnettes at the same time, there were ritualistic moments when compatriots felt compelled to take refuge behind the Lodge furniture.

And, bless him, the occultist can be as human and forgetful as the next person, despite the need for attention to detail. I remember a delightful occasion when, after an event which included the demonstration of certain yoga exercises, I went with the demonstrator, who was a truly lovely person in every sense of the word, to find refreshment after labour in a rather smart cocktail lounge. The beautiful demonstrator, feeling warm, was about to remove her top coat when she discovered she had nothing on but the skin-tight purple cat-suit in which she had demonstrated her exercises.

THE BROKEN WILL

So we all fumble along, in one way or another, gaining what comprehension we can from life's rhythms and rituals. For our habit patterns are in fact our own personal rituals. Until, at some time or other, the strength or our resolve or the kick of our desperation breaks us loose from our own individual ritualistic umbilical tower.

In his play *The Cocktail Party* the poet T. S. Eliot has a character remark:

> The self that can say 'I want this—or want that'—
> The self that wills—he is a feeble creature;
> He has to come to terms in the end
> With the obstinate, the tougher self; who does not speak
> Who never talks, who cannot argue;
> And who in some men may be the guardian—

This deep will of the guardian is the magician's sword of strength. But it has its imitator in self-will, and from this the deceptions of the magic of the shadow germinate. So let us consider will as the sorcerer's apprentice. It is in need of vocational training, but it is not a training that is gained merely by obeying rules.

In fact, one may very well ask, how is human will to be broken, in the sense that a thoroughbred horse is broken in order to be brought to the peak of its power without having its spirit destroyed? It is obviously in the unquenchable capacity of the human spirit that the secret of will is to be found.

Educators, psychologists and others have designed all sorts of games whereby people can experience the will. It is a perennial subject for philosophical debate. Dr. Assagioli, whose paper on techniques for training the will we previously quoted, has laid great emphasis on its development in his work on educational psychosynthesis. And those who feel they would like to experiment could make a start by looking through his book *Psychosynthesis: A Manual of Principles and Techniques.*

However, techniques are to a certain degree a matter of preference and opinion. We shall centre our study on the fundamental experiences which the techniques are intended to promote. Then it will be possible for the individual to decide whether life itself may not be putting him in the way of these experiences. And whether or not he wishes to employ this, that or the other technique, which he may have come across, in his encounter with experience.

As an example of the self-conditioning which our attitudes, and consequently our techniques of behaviour, impose, I have often quoted the delightful Groucho Marx incident from *A Night in Casablanca.* Having been given the ownership of an hotel, he ordered the manager to change all the numbers on the bedroom doors. 'Think of the confusion,' said the manager. 'No, think of the fun,' said Groucho.

In order to shift the gears of our attitudes we have to understand something of their mechanism. Those who can consciously accommodate the will of the guardian may not be innocents, but they retain some measure of innocency. They maintain an openness, even to the point of vulnerability, in their relationships. Even though some would think that this was a denial of will rather than its affirmation.

So often we associate will with precise, inviolate, authoritative knowledge and decision. And often it is hard enough to maintain strength of will and intention when we do in fact know where we are going. But have you considered the still greater resilience, the willing attitude towards life and events, which all of us need to muster when we don't know what the next move should be?

Living with the open question and maintaining the sensitivity of attitude which that requires can unfold a life-affirming willingness at quite a different level to the one which we normally associate with determination.

This is illustrated mythologically in some interpretations of the Parsifal legend. In her well-known book *From Ritual to Romance* the literary scholar Jessie Weston relates the tale of Parsifal's question.

On his first stumbling across the Grail Castle, Parsifal is dumbfounded and quite unable to appreciate the vision. He fails to ask the necessary magic question and the Castle vanishes. He finds himself back in the wilderness where an old woman reviles him for remaining dumb. Had he asked the right question of the vision before him, had he made a demand of his consciousness, the life-giving sustenance of the Grail Chalice would have flowed and fertility would have been restored to the land.

Parsifal is known as 'the fool made wise through pity'. And it is only after many years of wandering, during which his heart is touched by man's condition and he becomes sensible through compassion, that he manages to approach the Grail Castle once again. This time he does not remain dumb. And according to the legend which Jessie Weston has uncovered he asks the following question: 'Whom does the Grail serve?' In experiencing the answer the desert wilderness is made to flower.

Each one has to discover his own Grail question. And even though the form of it may vary it will take shape from within the depths of our essence. Rather like Peter's invocation, 'Whither goest thou, O Lord?' our own individual invocation will attract its answer only by being lived through. In other words, on registering our question we start to live with it and subsequently our life becomes the answer. For many people this may be some version of the simple demand, 'What am I?' or 'What is man?'.

Back behind what we are saying it is possible to see the outline of ancient magic rituals. In this form of invocation of our essence we have a psychological equivalent of the entry into temple, grove or lodge, with the demand for and provision of a password which will open the door to the sanctuary.

THE SACRIFICE

The next sequential stage is sacrifice. This links up with what we previously said about the individual Copernican revolution. It also brings us directly to our task of breaking the will. In a certain sense the purposeful and wilful individual lays himself on the altar.

However, in saying this we must also comment on contemporary interpretations of what sacrifice can mean. The word comes from the same root as the word 'sacred', which also means to make holy or whole, in the sense of being sanctified. In this sense, rather than requiring a giving up or cutting off, sacrifice entails taking something on. In practical terms maybe making time and energy available for new responsibilities. There may be some giving up because of this, but the emphasis is on the addition rather than the subtraction.

There is an aid—it really cannot be called a technique because the experience of it is such a private and individual matter—which can serve us here. This has been called the practice of harmlessness. For those who enjoy symbolism, it is the knife of sacrifice.

There is plenty to consider in this business of breaking the will. Confusion is easy. As we have said, it is completely different from breaking the spirit. It is really more a case of the technical development of the subtle parts of man's mechanism so that the spirit can be released or at least amplified.

Many of the magical rites of the ancient mysteries speak about initiation or the entry of man into new knowledge and understanding. This takes place when he has, so to speak, entered the temple for instruction and done sacrifice to the 'gods'. But some dreadful nonsense has been given out about the nature of initiation. And this has led to all sorts of egotism and foundationless psychological superiority. Let us be very simple about the whole subject and look at it in terms of our new recognition of sacrifice. A basic and commonsense approach to initiation lies in taking the noun 'initiate' and turning it into a verb 'through action'. In terms of life, people initiate themselves by initiating.

It is definitely not the purpose of the sacrifice and the

harmlessness that we are discussing to rob man of his initiative and attack, and the ageless wisdom of its teeth.

But having respect for the old truism that the means condition the end product, we should so order the initiatives we take that they do no harm. Now, think very carefully what this means. We often try to insult someone by saying, 'Oh, he's quite harmless'. However, the dentist, the surgeon or the doctor who removes something rotten or toxic from somebody does not do it with the intention of being harmful, does he? It is once again a question of motive and attitude. In undertaking a particular action are we being thoughtful or considerate of the whole situation in so far as we understand it?

Harmlessness is, of course, far more than not causing wanton indiscriminate destruction. In its essential nature it is a business of creative economy. Because the harmless person will recognise that the substance in the storehouse of the universe can have many uses. That which may feed another should not be dissipated simply because it does not appeal to personal taste.

This outlook is different from a purely *laissez-faire* attitude, which is often simply a lazy attitude. It involves some attempt to understand what is meant for what. We will go further into this when we touch on the subject of relationships and ecology in the next chapter.

Those who find it easier to look at things in categories or under subheadings can take a glance at the relative harmlessness of their approach to action in terms of:

(a) Harmlessness in thought, involving all that we perpetrate in terms of relaying vicious criticism, scandal and hate.

(b) Harmlessness in emotion. The olden-day witches

were often accused of ill-wishing person or property. But if we are frank in our observation, how often have we, under the influence of contrary emotion, played the same game?

(c) Harmlessness in act. This is probably the easiest category to observe because viciousness has been concretised and becomes unmistakably noticeable. But when we do notice it we should trace it back and see how it is motivated from the other two levels.

A well-meaning moralistic hopefulness will not take us too far in this observation of ourselves. It is all very well to say we do not want to be unkind and then attempt to cultivate kindness. We know that this in unlikely to be completely successful because from our study of duality we know that we cannot humanly hold the pendulum of action permanently back in one position.

Initially we have to take a hard look at all these things. Just see exactly how the energy that flows through us is used to hurt and harm. Because until we understand what is going on in ourselves there is little chance of employing this energy in any other way.

In due season such observation can give us a fighting chance of achieving some conversion of energy and the scene takes on a different character. And later, when we look back, this conversion in ourselves may seem to be magical and simple, because what we have attempted from below has been aided from above, and the whole event has had the subtle delicacy of a growing plant. Unbridled destructive emotion understood and converted can become the fuel of imagination, and vitalised imagination is an employee of initiative. And in initiated action comes further knowledge and understanding, which in its turn is the usher to wisdom. The fantastic examples of people like Helen Keller are the witnesses of this.

THE INNOCENT HEART

Taken in this sense harmlessness is Parsifal's compassion, which made him wise.

It is after having gone through this experience of entering the temple and of dedicating the will through the melting of our hearts in sacrifice that we can go on to a proper study of the more technical aspects of so-called magic. It is unfortunate that a great deal of magical study only begins at this point, having given a cursory glance at what is considered a symbolic purification. In fact the sort of purification which we have discussed is our recognition that we, within ourselves, work with the dirt of the earth before it or us can ever be holy!

Purification in this sense of the awakening or reawakening of a heart-melting innocency has nothing to do with an off-putting puritanical attitude. There is a sort of psychic stripping down to essentials, which is not rejection because each psychological garment we employ is seen for what it is, valued for what it is, and when necessary let go for what it is. It is rather like the scene towards the end of Ibsen's famous play where Peer Gynt peels the onion. The Button-moulder has met Peer Gynt at the end of his life and has questioned him on what he is. He has asked him why he should not be melted down to be remade. And Peer sits and peels an onion to find his heart. Skin after skin of the onion's substance falls to the floor. Like Peer, at the end of our peeling we may appear to be left with annihilating nothingness. But it is in that moment of desperate empty aloneness that he hears the song of his waiting sweetheart Solve, like the voice of his soul, and finds his way. She represents his hidden guardian waiting for him to return from his wanderings. Similarly when we seem internally to be without trappings and there appears to be only a void, then, as the heart calls out, there can exist a type of vacuum which the transcendental energy of the other universe can fill.

This is very hard to describe. It is not blankness or psychic negativity. It is not a case of throwing the devil out of our psychic house so that the proverbial seven other devils can have squatters' rights to set up an anarchic commune. Because this particular kind of vacuum or way-making, this essential openness of heart, is really initiated at a formless level. It may affect the form, the psychic and psychological onion skins which seem to hide it, but which really don't (even though we have to work at the peeling) because it is not of their substance. This clearing, this open space, is not of any of our form worlds.

Human consciousness has the capacity to experience that which is formless and timeless. In the midst of self-observation and the observation of the natural world, and because of our location in time and space, we have to provide the bridge between our universe and the other one. This bridge-building is our special human function. And because of it our creativity can be blessed with an infinite magical potential, literally by the grace of God.

MECHANICS OF MAGIC

An inner re-orientation is like a fresh charge of energy. When revolution takes place within us to any marked extent the outward result can be like re-programming a magnetic tape. The fresh charge can de-magnetise the old programme and allow the recording of a new one, according to the way in which we are tuned for reception.

Here our own special bias of mental attention plays its part. But response to the fresh energy flow comes from several areas of our mechanism, as well as the mind. Earlier we mentioned the conversion of erratic emotional forces into constructive imagination, and this is one of the elements which can rise up to support the new activity. The art of magical visualisation is a natural practice, an automatic reaction of our mechanism. All of us build pictures in the mind's eye, which is an elementary stage of visualisation. However, the major proportion of this subjective activity is the result of memories stimulated by past experience. We build on that which is already old. We regurgitate old forms which are already set with their own particular emotional colouring. It is only rarely that we accept new light from within ourselves and respond by constructing a blueprint which is at least original in terms of our own conscious experience.

However, when we do break new ground for ourselves we stand a chance of pathfinding for our neighbour as well. True magicians, in the deeper sense of the name, are blessed with a certain gift of originality, in that they become pioneers of the territory, if we may call it that, of the other universe.

In her book on meditation and its practice, called *The Silent Path*, M. J. Eastcott discusses the use of visual imagination in very simple terms in the chapter 'The Foot of the Stairway'.

This subjective building work is one of the means of aligning the outer with the inner. At the border of the formless universe there is a sort of intuitive response in consciousness to the inner charge of new energy. This stirring in turn triggers mental construction which initiates a blueprint for action. This provides a sort of personal platonic-style form. Furthermore, detailed mental response to this constructs a more concrete plan, which corresponds to the picture-building stage we spoke of earlier. This in turn is buttressed by emotional, imaginative support. The various ramifications of the plan are filled in. Then, if the vortex of this activity is sufficiently strong and magnetic, it draws more tangible vitality to itself, possibly in the shape of finance or whatever else is necessary for it finally to precipitate on to the physical level. There, if attention is sustained, one has a final putting together of component parts in physical matter.

This sequence of clothing is followed through whether we are discussing individual or community activity. The mental, emotional and physical support for the plan may come from the resources of one individual or many. In either case, let us look some more at what is involved in raising that support.

We have already mentioned visualisation and the fact that it is not just picture-building. It starts with the intuitive sensing of the inner impulse. And this is made possible by the earlier preparation of heart-melting, which is necessary if we are to go beyond the mind, and also subsequently have the mind provide some spontaneous images which are not inevitably the material of our usual personal clichés. Sometimes the mind, galvanised into rummaging in its cellars and attics, may throw up surprising symbols such as it does in the dream state of sleep.

At first our response to the new energy may be no

more than a sense of impression. But as visualisation gets under way we may see some clear picture quite spontaneously, almost like a form of mental clairvoyance, but this is not necessarily so with everyone. And as these visions or concepts grow strong they evoke, as we have pointed out, a natural mental-emotional response.

When this happens colour often plays a significant part in representing differing qualities of substance. The research works which deal with the psychological aspects of colour usually list commonly accepted interpretations of various colours, some of which are part of colloquial language. A red fury, a dark blue mood or a green signal are most obvious examples. However, the use of colour in visualisation can often be highly personal.

One has only to go through the various world religions to see that at some time or other most colours have had sacred significance to some group of people. Priests and monks wear different-coloured robes according to faith. In certain churches the colour of altar cloths, hangings or vestments is changed to represent different church festivals.

The different effect of colours, according to the psychic state of those exposed to them, has been noted by many investigators. Deutsch, for instance, points out in *Colour Psychology and Colour Therapy* that there is a reflex action in the vascular system and a possible organic change, even if only indirectly through the emotional nature. In the use of various coloured lighting as a means of therapy Deutsch states: 'The psychic process which is brought into play here is easily stated: the coloured light changes the environment. Through the changed appearance of the environment, the individual is lifted out of reality.'

Of course, much of the individual response to colour is conditioned by memory. Different colours associate with various half-recollected scenes and these in turn connect us with previous experience. In magical visualisation one must understand this, and get behind the situation so that it does not take over and sway one with its outer appearance. For one recognises that the inner impulsing energy which we have spoken of is a light which becomes clothed with colour to fulfil its purpose, rather than just being used to show off the array of colours which we have already collected within our personal aura.

That this whole subject is intensely practical in material terms is illustrated by the amount of study given to it by such branches of marketing as the packaging industry. One type of coloured packet design will attract a customer to a specific kind of commodity, while another will not.

Another line of psychological/psychic study which relates to this and to the precipitation of an inner blueprint on to the level of material existence is the correspondence between colour and sound.

Concerning the nature of sound and its quality, D. H. Andrews in his book *Radiant Symphony* has gone as far as to say that 'the universe is made up not of matter but of music'. He sets out to show in terms of objective observation something that Richard Wagner tried to portray in his music dramas, that each person and object has its *leit-motiv*, keynote or special sound-wave.

This brings us on to the business of projecting, or sending forth on a word, the thought-forms created through visualisation.

THE USE OF SOUND

If one likens the whole enterprise to the work of an architect, there is the initial concept of the ground plan, then the builders are called in to construct according to plan in the appropriate material, and finally there comes the time for selling or using the building.

While the first stage will proceed in silence, aside from some reflective consultation, sound will play a part in the second and third stages. First in a magnetic sense to call in the builders and assemble material for their use. And second in a radiant way to project the construction or put it on the market, as it were.

In terms of subjective work there is a fascinating area of study in relation to rhythmic prayer, invocation and mantras. It is part of the more subtle side of ritual. In different eras of history sound has been used according to the conventions and understanding of the time. Fables bring rumours of its supposed use in the construction of great edifices such as Stonehenge and the Pyramids. Of course, while fables usually carry a grain of truth they are also likely to be considerably embroidered as the years go by. Major revelation in the uses of sound lies before us in the future. Both in terms of what may be done by machines working through super- or sub-sonic wavelengths, and also in terms of the rediscovery and contemporary adaptation of ancient occult sound formulas. Indeed, the former may be something of an externalisation of the latter.

Chants and invocations have been used in all ages to evoke a particular sensation or attitude in the followers of a cause. These sensations may range all the way from the contemplative quiet of a monastery Te Deum to the furious Sieg Heil of a Nazi rally. In Japan one of the brands of new Buddhism to which many young people are responding is employing mass chanting in its devotions.

Currently, a number of schools of mantra meditation, well known in the East for many years, have spread rapidly in the West. The focusing and opening of the mind towards the transcendental is based on the use of traditional mantramic sound, which need not of course be vocalised but can be sounded mentally. It is true that such mantras repeated rhythmically can have a definite effect on the psyche and that for many they represent a helpful speeding-up process, which although ancient is in key with modern times. However, the point has been made by some observers that such speeding up can bring about a form of psychic indigestion in the unprepared which slower methods involving understanding and self-observation and the gradual development of a sense of purpose and spiritual identity are less likely to do. But in this, as in other things, man has claimed his life-given right to experiment. General rules cannot be made, it is a matter of what could be called psychic metabolism in relation to the mechanics of magic. The thing to recollect, as we stressed earlier, is that all these means to an end are in fact part of mechanics. They may be doors and keys to doors, but they are not the magical stuff of life itself.

The traditions of the ageless wisdom maintain that there exist powerful invocative mantrams for different objectives, but that these are guarded and secret. Mankind's collective consciousness is as yet too near his animal nature and his behaviour turns out too mean and too naturally violent to be trusted with what are, in effect, like the lost sound of masonry, words of power. The flame-like vitality invoked by such sounds could, it is maintained, destroy just as much as they could create if employed where their vehicle or human sounding-box were unprepared and unresilient. The tale of Semile and Jupiter is echoed here. And, anyway, whether these tales contain truth or not, one has only to consider the incredible and uncontrolled racket of noise which distinguishes most large centres of human population to appreciate that we have some way to go in learning about the controlled use of sound. Noise abatement societies are a fairly recent institution, and are mainly set up to deal with the end-effect.

None the less, certain sorts of power-words are already with us and in public use. Not, of course, that the words themselves have any mysterious power, but the use of them in a specific way has a seemingly powerful outer effect. And if these mantras were not effective one would not find so many highly paid executives employed to study and construct them. I refer to the use of slogan in politics, business advertising and the general administration of public life.

There have been many psychological investigations into the effects of brain-washing recently. And books like Sargent's *Battle for the Mind* and Packard's *The Hidden Persuaders* have received a lot of publicity in their time. Once awakened and alert to the significance of slogans, and sometimes through sheer over-exposure, the human being is quite capable of developing resistance or of just letting them slide by. But there are obvious dangers. The use of sound in battles of words is well known to the filibustering dictator and the more subtle political manipulator.

Quite aside from so-called words of power it is an easy step to recognise the powerful energy that can be carried by words in general. Whether used vocally or in terms of written or pictured symbol these are man's basic means of communication. The effect of great literature is obvious. But look also at the premium placed by politician, artist and business man on the truly skilled script-writer. Such authors are strong allies in the magical effect these people want to convey.

In fact, understanding the value and use of speech is a primary lesson in the mechanics of magic. Follow this by linking the use of speech with what we previously said about the practice of harmlessness, and just see how it can help a very definite and practical shift in relationship to one's whole environment. If God really is love, and if we have any sort of contact with the other universe from which love issues, then we also have some capacity in our ability to communicate to let loose the murmur of love in this world. And in doing this men learn to sing with Krishna.

A perceptive understanding of the use of speech is really a matter of attention. And attention is an aspect of will, which is what we set out to discuss in this chapter.

Dr. Assagioli, whose work on psychosynthesis has already been referred to, quotes a statement by Coué, who made extensive studies in auto-suggestion: 'When the will and the imagination are in conflict, the imagination always wins.' Attention can be one of the aids in getting through this conflict. How many people have managed to bring about order in the storm of some emotional crisis when the imagination is in riot, by the device of attending with precision to some simple task. Gardening, carpentry and the washing-up have helped many people in the moment of turmoil.

PSYCHIC UNFOLDMENT

This type of attention is not any rigid blinkered form of concentration, but rather a sensitive inner alertness coupled to a clear focus on what one is doing. If experienced frequently it has an inevitable effect upon the whole psyche, and brings about a consequent psychic development.

So often in relation to psychic things people think only of a narrow band of rather concrete phenomena; seeing a ghost, hearing a voice or materialising an apport (that is the transfer of a physical object from one place to another at a higher energy frequency than is customary for the object, so that it seemingly materialises in a closed room). Such phenomenal activity may be the gift of certain specially trained or endowed people. But most human beings are capable of a whole range of subtle, if less sensational, development.

Nowadays it is becoming fashionable to speak of 'sensitivity training'. We have already mentioned our capacity for deep intuitive awakening to inner impressions, and this has an outer correspondence in that fine sensitivity to the real need of people, regardless of what they may be saying or doing, which a few people display. At the moment this particular psychic gift is probably more rare than that seeing of astral phenomena which we usually think of as being the gift of clairvoyance.

Inevitably there are many ways in which we learn to

see or feel behind appearances. A good interviewer, whether in journalism, business or whatever, is said to develop a nose for truth. But the preparations for magic which culminate in heart-melting prepare us for life's sensitivity training as well.

Another similar, subtle psychic unfoldment is related to right timing. We already mentioned human consciousness as being a link between a timeless state and our usual time sequence. Because of this some people develop a beautiful sense of the seasons and cycles of their own and other people's lives. This is not the same as sensing the sort of subjective time-belt which we all play with to some extent, saying this is long and that is short according to our emotional reaction to the pleasure and pain of the moment. More often than not in such cases we let ourselves be most terribly hypnotised by the calendar, particularly in relation to what is expected of us at such and such an age. Right timing could be thought of as an inner sense of rhythm. And there are people who have built splendid careers on their psychic sense of timing, which has prompted them to be in the right place at the right time or to make the correct telephone call at the precisely needed hour.

An inner sense of cycles is probably awakening in a larger number of people than we realise. This psychic sensitivity concerns the basic tides of our life experience. It can help people foster a sense of serene acceptance when life moves them seemingly irrevocably from one set of experiences to another. And, if the move truly constitutes part of a new cycle for them, it can introduce them to its significance.

Many mystics have spoken or written of a basic meditation experience, which they have sought to convey in the concept that 'GOD IS'. Several occult treatises maintain the idea that the master guardians of the world adopt a similar focus of consciousness when great cycles of human civilisation, which they have worked to build and enhance, fulfil their usefulness and are swept away in the avalanche of change which often precedes a new construction which will be more adapted to the developments that have taken place in human outlook. Behind the change, the new developments and all their dualistic vicissitudes life eternal is represented by the timeless omnipotence of deity. And in the experience of meditation we touch something which we might as well call 'the freedom of time' when we are introduced to something which is beyond time's reach.

Telepathy is one more of the general psychic sensitivities which hover on the brink of many people's recognised capacities. In the main, such indication of telepathy that there is is haphazard, unpredictable and quite outside conscious control. Gilbert Murray did some research on this in the early part of the century, which has been variously reported. A brief account of his work is to be found in Raynor Johnston's book on psychic research, published in the Teach Yourself series which is brought out in the U.K. This is helpful for getting a bird's-eye view of the subject by means of some quick reading. Rhine's statistical work, mainly undertaken at Duke University, is well known. And it is reported that in the future Sir Alistair Hardy's project for 'Research into Religious Experience' at Manchester College, Oxford, may possibly take a look at telepathic experience if research funds permit.

It is certain that a great deal of patient objective work is required on the subject of telepathy. Not only to prove that it happens to the satisfaction of a hard-headed world, but in order to understand the mechanics of how it happens. Is it an activity of mind functioning entirely through the brain-waves, which in material terms seem to be fairly weak? Or are there possibly a variety of different types of telepathy, using different energy centres and consequently different parts of the glandular system, according to whether the sending is emotionally, mentally or intuitively impulsed? There is also the possibility that some telepathy by-passes man's physical vehicle altogether.

One valuable research field is to be found among practising psychics, although these people have often been exploited and abused, and are generally timid of what they think research conditions will imply. A good many professional sensitives have a marked telepathic capacity; with some it is even their major gift. However, as a fair number of those in public work are naturally enough tied in with the large orthodox spiritualist movement and, as the avowed service objective of this movement is to prove that death is not the end of human experience, mediums are often at pains to discount their telepathic gifts. But while telepathy is not considered to be clairvoyance or clairaudience in the generally accepted sense it is not to be belittled and is probably one of the ways available to us for contact both with the animal kingdom and also with insubstantial realms of life. It is also a valuable asset in consultation work. In fact many of the worried members of the public who consult mediums go for general advice and are not necessarily insisting that survival be proved to them.

This suggestion is not, of course, an attempt to take the teeth out of the spiritualist movement but to add to the range of its recognised services. Provided the public know in advance what they are booking for, an hour's consultation with a sensitive telepath could be a more valuable experience than an interview with a medium who is on the defensive and under obligation to produce dear old Uncle George. Mind you, one consideration in relation to this is that many mediums use several gifts, just as each of us uses several senses at once, and switch back and forth without precisely knowing which psychic ability they employ in the heat of the moment.

If in the future research services can make an objective study of psychic phenomena, with some reference to basic psychological knowledge, we could have an interesting shift of attitude. The College of Psychic Studies in London is an organisation interested in both psychological and psychic phenomena, which is trying to encourage new lines of investigation.

Sensitivity training is likely to be a subtle business for most people. We may be irritated by the fog that surrounds the subject of psychic research, but when the prospect is unclear are we not being challenged by life to walk watchfully? So we just have to proceed with willing attention. And sometimes, usually in their own good time and for a good reason, the more startling and dramatic psychic events do happen along the way.

I remember one close friend of mine telling me a few years before the end of her full and useful life how she had gone into a well-known London church to attend the Eucharist one Sunday morning. As the priest came forward from the altar and held out the sacrament, she started up from her knees to take communion with the rest of the congregation. Suddenly she observed that what one might call the proscenium arch of the church, in front of the altar area, was misting over. Although she had some small experience of psychic phenomena, nothing of that nature was in her thoughts at the time. Somewhat surprised, but with a curious tingle of expectancy alerted in her, she remained on her knees in an attitude of prayer. The mist continued to densify till priest and congregation were lost from view and the area had become to all intents and purposes a cinema screen.

On to this screen scenes from her life were projected. These vignettes were particularly explanatory of the key relationships in her life. And furthermore they were not confined to a particular incarnation but stretched back in time providing illustrations from several existences. One character's life thread stretched through most of the sequence of time with her own, and much relating to love and antipathy became plain. At least one traumatic death experience was shown when a group of people had been tied naked to a raft and slowly drowned. Certain of the locations in various countries were recognisable. And a sort of inner intuitive commentary seemed to be explaining the value of what was taking place. But other places bore no resemblance to anything recognised by the mind of her present personality. And as the time belt extended back further and further through the centuries, the pictures developed a wobbling, fluctuating quality as though seen through disturbed water. Eventually, they faded out and the mist which had provided the screen for their transmission evaporated. This occurred just as the priest completed giving the sacrament and the last members of the congregation returned from the altar.

The subject of this extraordinary experience was still on her knees and although a new calm of spirit had been born in her because much had been explained, she was understandably weeping as a result of the emotional impact of what she had seen. She told practically no one of the experience. It was deeply personal and private, and there was no reason to convince anyone else of its authenticity. In mentioning it to a few intimates, it could only be told on the basis of such and such was experienced by me, take it or leave it, as you wish. Now that she has passed on, it seems just and right to use it as an illustration.

Another private experience which one may now pass on was told me by a rather well-known personality. His line of work was well defined and he never publicly spoke about such experiences or ever encouraged people to investigate psychic phenomena. He took the point of view that such events took place in due season when required by the holy spirit.

It was the custom of this friend to practise brief relaxed moments of recollection or meditation when he would register the spiritual identity back behind his outer appearance. But at one stage in his spiritual studies he found himself shaken awake early in the morning, and impelled to meditate. During one of these experiences, in the course of an absorbing meditation, he found himself transported in consciousness to a remarkable, open-columned building. There he took part in a ritual ceremony which he said was not unlike masonic practice, though he did not fully explain what significance this form of service had for him. A great many people were present, either taking part or as spectators, inside or outside the building. In his estimation he mentioned a figure of about three thousand, though with this sort of quantity accuracy was obviously impossible.

A good few years later when he was visiting Athens for the first time he went to pay his respects to a certain well-known ruin. There he had the shock of recognising where he had been, though the building he had entered in meditation had been in a pristine state of preservation.

An interesting sidelight on this curious experience is the possibility that some of the greatest material monuments of different high points of civilisation are precipitations of buildings already perfected and in use in more subtle estates of life. We are all only too familiar with the sensation that our actions, projects and materialisations do not measure up even to our own necessarily limited concept of them. But if our philosophy of magic has a spark of truth in it is it not possible that there are times in our collective history, as well as in our personal lives, when the inner and the outer worlds are aligned in harmony? And when this happens things of an archetypal nature find agents capable of anchoring at least their material replica on earth. And these stand as emblems of glory and encouragement to all mankind. So something of the essential quality which inspired the archetype or platonic-form gets anchored as well.

Something similar to my friend's experience is often mentioned in theosophical and other occult literature. It is usually presented as the concept that some people attend night-school, in the sense that while the physical body sleeps the consciousness in subtler form will find instructors or take part in projects in another realm. Unfortunately, it would seem that the physical brain is reluctant to register an experience in which it has not participated. Consequently there is little or no continuity of consciousness when we return to the physical mechanism whatever may be impressed on the more subtle parts of our nature.

However, in Dr. Karagulla's book *Breakthrough to Creativity* we find an account of a subject who was able to recall something about such class-work. The person concerned recognised continuity. That is on different occasions she registered being in the same place and in the presence of the same people, not known to her in waking consciousness. She also recollected some material of a scientific nature given to her and made some notes on waking. At the time of this account of Dr. Karagulla's investigation going to press this was being evaluated.

SYNTHESIS

Obviously man's psychological and psychic nature is capable of multifarious experience. The ramifications of our make-up, and the many different levels and qualities of energy with which we are capable of working, seem endless. And it is perfectly possible to become fascinated by the kaleidoscope of our own nature to such a degree that for a long time we move no more. We get lost in the highways and byways of us.

But eventually minor drives and objectives lose their intensity and we come back to our central question about the purpose of life. Like Parsifal we ask about the Grail. We go through the experience of heart-melting again and again. And the tough, inner guardian has a chance to exercise that peaceful, silent will to love.

If this did not occur what future would man have? As a creative being with incredible energy at his disposal is he to chase one selfish goal after another *ad infinitum*? In this prospect is he not the black magician in embryo? And in this sense are we not all potential black magicians? Until we decide to work with the synthesising influence of the other universe, under whatever name we care to call it, and give the many fragments of our nature a chance to find their right relation to each other.

In Wagner's version of the Parsifal story one of the characters portrays our vacillation and its ending in a commitment which changes everything. In the music drama *Parsifal*, Kundry is a strange woman representing all the volatile psychic passion of human nature. Her time is divided. Sometimes she performs errands for the knights of the Holy Grail. On other occasions she is summoned by Klingsor, the master of dark sorcery, who seeks the Grail power for himself. Kundry is a go-between. At one moment she is carrying balm to the wounded Grail King, Amfortas. And when we see her next she is transformed at Klingsor's behest into a seductress who can lure the Grail knights from their charge. Yet it is her kiss that pierces Parsifal's heart, making him recollect his origin, and causing the black magician's kingdom to dissolve. Later when Parsifal is master of compassion, and anointed future Grail King, he baptises Kundry. Then her wild and tortured cries are replaced by the single word 'service'. In the Grail service she discovers peace and ends her dualistic existence.

Service is an overworked word. But it is a simple one.

And it means a lot in terms of love and givingness. Behind its many forms and faces there lies goodwill. And this other simple word, often glibly spoken, is a key to creative magic. Goodwill is the hope awoken by vision and by love. And it is the dynamic charge that manifests in men who have breathed the atmosphere of the other universe.

Stop for one moment and imagine what would be the effect of mass goodwill channelled by many millions of human beings who recognised themselves as potential magicians. Our civilisation could be transfigured. We could touch a glory and know freedom quite beyond our own manufacture. In our heart of hearts we know the angels' Christmas song carries truth and justice and can be prophetic. But there must be goodwill towards men before there can be peace on earth. Why should we expect to get it the other way round?

These inner experiences which may sound mystic, vague or poetic when written about, are really of tremendous practical importance. When, either through observation of nature or experience in meditation, a sense of the wholeness of life is born in the individual his attitude is changed fundamentally. The recognition of an innate sense of synthesis means that all relationships are seen in a new light.

3 *The Lord of Civilisation*

AQUARIUS

Tides and cycles overlap in such a way that human history is always involved in some sort of turning point. Which, of course, gives historians delightful scope for analysis. Perhaps one day the story of the evolution of human consciousness will be written. Then, no doubt, major events will be evaluated very differently from the way in which they are often presented now. Although some of today's history analysts have got free from the more partisan approach of former times. Just after I gave a talk somewhere or other someone once handed me a slip of paper with the following perceptive statement on it. Though no reference was given it was attributed to the wisdom of Arnold Toynbee.

> My own guess is that our age will be remembered chiefly, neither for its horrifying crimes nor for its astonishing inventions, but for having been the first age, since the dawn of civilisation, in which people dared to think it practicable to make the ideal of welfare for all a practical objective instead of a mere Utopian dream.

To my mind, this development points up the astonishing growth of public goodwill, uniting as it does qualities of heart and head on a wide scale. And the huge reservoir of latent goodwill needed for this trend to start showing above the surface of man's subjective life is the warranty that a great deal of creative magic is possible in many departments of life. Where goodwill is not in circulation we know that life can be grim indeed.

Professor Paolo Rossi, in his book *Francis Bacon; From Magic to Science*, makes interesting comments on what some people have called the English renaissance and others look on as the birthing of modern scientific method. At one point in his work he quotes Bacon's writing:

> Astrology, natural magic, and alchemy, of which sciences nevertheless the ends and pretences are noble . . . but the derivations and prosecutions to these ends both in theories and in practices are full of error and vanity.

Rossi then goes on to comment on this statement:

> According to Bacon, magic endeavours to dominate and to improve nature; and for this it should be imitated. Where it needs revising is in its claim to use one man's inspiration instead of the organised efforts of the human race, and to make science serve individual ends rather than mankind.

This seems to me to be a succinct way of putting what we have said about the distinction between creative magic and the shadow play of selfishness. It also illustrates very well how creativity motivated by a steadfast goodwill is part of the essential foundation for human maturity. And while it is true each human individual may be in embryo an unconscious black magician, he is also a potential creative magician whose stature can increase through work for the general good.

Right now we are in a moment of time where former

social frontiers have been smashed up around us. Sheltered cultures that thrived in protected areas of society have been split wide open. Modern communications and transport simply require feeding with XYZ units of financial energy to bring any part of the free world and a lot of the rest of it within our individual range. And we are being forced by the pressure of history, whether the thought is distasteful or not, to consider civilisation in pan-humanistic terms. Man is being called to a collective magical act—the creation of a new world civilisation.

This prospect is so immense that conceivable results seem as if they must be far distant in time. And our immediate problems seem so overwhelmingly on top of us that they block any comprehensive vision of the horizon. But there is nothing unusual or unnatural in this. It is just another sort of challenge. The apprentice of creative magic often has a sticky start because he is inevitably faced with the full force of world illusion. And whether collective or personal a very large proportion of our problems are the children of some sort of illusion.

One thing that the metaphysical churches and groups have always stressed is the need to look beyond appearances to the essence. And in doing so they have set the stage for a healthy approach to creative magic.

Shortly before he passed from the physical scene the psychiatrist Carl Jung issued a newspaper article in which he examined some of the psychological implications of astrological symbolism as this applied to various phases of civilisation. He saw the symbolism covering deep psychological changes of tide within the collective consciousness. And he mentioned the widespread belief that humanity was transiting into a 2,000-year period governed by qualities emblemised in the Aquarian water-carrier, who is said to bring the waters of life to thirsty men.

Although the early Christians employed, as 'fishers of men', the symbol of the fish which stood for the age of Pisces, out of which we are now travelling, there are many people who believe that Christ foresaw the consummation of His work in the age of Aquarius. It is recorded that He prophetically guided His disciples to the house where they were to prepare for the communion feast, by telling them to watch for the man bearing the pitcher of water. Certainly it is in the example of the shared communion that we can find an essential core around which to build an Aquarian civilisation. And not only in a mystical sense. The principle of sharing offers a plain and vital clue to economic survival on a world scale.

If the two symbols of communion, wine representing blood or life and bread representing body or substance, are to be shared by all men, then man, as he now is, will certainly have to stretch and grow.

Sometimes one hears sharp criticism of space-exploration programmes which devour financial resources. This money in the opinion of the critics could be put to much better trouble-curing use at home. And, as we know, both the Americans and Russians seem to have cut back their space programmes recently. However, I wonder if the efforts to reach out into the solar system are not in themselves a symbolic indication of man's intent to achieve the necessary stretch in consciousness, a tangible emblem of a new attempt to touch what mystics like Bucke have termed cosmic consciousness.

During the course of a television discussion shortly after the first moon landing the economist Barbara Ward made a point about financing space research. She said that on the figures available at the time the money spent on space research in the U.S.A. was approximately 1 per cent of the national income, whereas the total spent on the requirements of warfare, armaments and general military activity came to around some 40 per cent. And in the face of this huge figure the space programme could hardly be called a haemorrhage of waste, whatever one's point of view. In so far as it helps to raise man's sights, it can prove a blessing, and need not cripple social relief programmes. In fact, given public will to accomplish, both can be taken care of.

ECOLOGY

If we stand at least a fighting chance of being drawn upward in growth by some sort of extended vision, like a plant is drawn towards the sun, then it is also true that we are being forced from below. The sheer pressures of life on earth are seeing to this. The numerical weight of our present global population and the problems of supplying it with necessities are making us stretch our outlook. Ecology has become one of the new in-words.

According to John Davy, the journalist and educator, this is the study of the relationship between living groups. This naturally includes a pan-humanistic approach to life, but can also involve both subhuman and superhuman expressions of living energy. Everything has to be taken into account as part of a living whole. Whatever we look at we must consider it as another aspect of 'that in which we live and move and have our being', however disagreeable this thought may be to our myopic pride.

I first came across the term ecology in the context of a novel called *Dune*, which was dedicated by the author to all planetary ecologists. It concerned a largely desert world where every morsel of food and every drop of moisture was so vital to the preservation of life that the native desert-dwellers had to preserve and transform their own sweat in order to survive. We do not live in such a desert and the phrase 'by the sweat of our brow' does not have to be taken quite so literally. However, we could quite rapidly transform large sections of the habitable globe into toxic wasteland unless we take the study of ecology, and subsidiary problems of population and pollution, very seriously. The nettle is still within our grasp.

It is often the case that where we are too inert or obtuse to respond to vision some economic factor will create an uncomfortable friction which forces us to move on. And in fact on the world scale, if we take an instance like the emancipation of women, economic necessity stimulated by two world wars has probably achieved more than political agitation, although this certainly played a highly important role in highlighting the way things obviously had to develop.

In moments of economic crisis during recent years some commentators have suggested that we abandon all attempt to live by a 'gold standard'. Some of our attitudes to money are very subjective. While most sensible people use it not for its own sake but for what it is worth in terms of supply and services, the idea that the love of money is the root of evil harks back to Albricht's curse,

Albricht being Wagner's dwarf who forswore all love in order to possess the Rhinegold.

Certainly we tend to protect and almost worship this metal most curiously. We laboriously dig it from one hole in the ground and then like industrious squirrels we promptly hide it away in another. Is this use of gold really suited to the new Aquarian way of life?

As we learn more about the fundamental allness of energy and regard it as the factual basis for a proper study of ecology, and incidentally for magic too, perhaps we will learn to reckon treasure in terms of energy units, with money being just one of the many forms in which energy can be concretised. We will return gold to the Rhine or general flow of life, knowing that it cannot be thought of as being in any way separate from the circulation of that flow.

However, it may well be fortunate that many of our problems are not resolved too soon. We have so much to learn. We are often eager to force a situation that seems disruptive, back into the confining pattern of some *status quo* which feels safe because it is familiar, whereas in holding the situation open there is a chance of getting some glimpse of an entirely new prospect.

CO-OPERATION

This holding of a growing-space is a tricky accomplishment. We all realise that there are moments of crisis where someone has to take hold of a situation very firmly. In a wild and fluid predicament during some group activity there may come a period where someone will, in the heat of the moment, take command and issue instructions all round. If a common disaster is seen by all to have been averted or an achievement gained by such action, then there is gratitude for timely leadership. But if members of say a family or other similar group rely on a boss to make decisions for them in regions where they actually have capacity and opportunity to work things out for themselves or in co-operation, and especially if this comes about because of their inertia or weakness, then the situation is not so healthy.

In the best sort of human combine it is a truism that everyone should be strong and self-respecting at their own level and in terms of their chosen function, whatever it be. There may be a hierarchy of administration, but it is a hierarchy which is ideally built on mutual co-operation rather than on any sort of totalitarian domination.

We do not always recognise this balance of function working out in our everyday environment. The changes of emphasis in relationships are often very slight from day to day. But when things go sour on the grand scale, perhaps in an international sense, we all know the horror of the consequences. In a time of fluidity and constant crisis it is easy to submit to dictatorship of some sort for the sake of what feels like the comfort of a firm guiding hand. And at first such totalitarian influence may seem to come as a blessed relief after a period of seeming chaos. History records the beguiling effect of some of Hitler's initial reforms when he was installed as Führer figure. His back-handed employment of Aquarian principles such as 'strength through joy' further disguised the sinister effect of totalitarian action, which, in the long run, always means the smotheration of essential human-spiritedness.

Today we are all involved in huge changes both in our

psyche and in our civilisation. It is small wonder that human leadership seems to vacillate, often to a point where the ordinary well-meaning citizen is in a state of considerable frustration and exasperation. But totalitarian dictatorship from any direction, whatever it may be believed to have achieved in the past, is not the answer. The human spirit requires freedom if there is to be any hope of it ever achieving mature expression.

Certainly the impact of energies which nearly every community in the world is receiving today needs digesting and this requires a lot of magical transformation work. But turning people into parts of a regimented mechanism will only appear to do the trick for a relatively short period.

One of the potential glories of the human species is its tremendous variety. This complex asset makes the task of maturing a world civilisation particularly difficult. But to go back to our starting point of the confrontation between the King and the barons, representing life and consciousness, we have to re-establish Magna Carta in topical form all the time in order to make freedom live.

Every day, somewhere, brave men and women are facing seemingly impossible challenges of all sorts and are succeeding in bringing creative solutions literally out of thin air. And when they do so they are playing their part in meditating through into the everyday world a civilisation inspired to some degree from the unseen universe. This is magic.

The large public funds of goodwill which are latent in the human heart need to be awoken and marshalled. One might almost say that goodwill needs to be organised, but this has become something of a dirty word in certain contexts. And there is a well-known story of a young devil going in panic to an older devil to tell him that he had just seen a man pick up a bit of truth. What was to be done about it? 'Nothing,' said the old devil, 'give him time and he'll try to organise it and that will create more havoc than you and I and a thousand like us could possibly provoke.'

However, there can be a difference between the totalitarian regimentation which we have just discussed and organisation. In its real sense the understanding of the word 'organise', which comes from the same root as organic, means an appreciation of tides and seasons and the inherent function of things. The dictionary cites a Greek word *organon* as being the parent of organ, organic, organism and organise. The parent word meant literally a tool or instrument, and nowadays when it is used it is considered to mean 'an instrument of thought' or 'a system of logic'.

THE ORGANONS

The energy of dynamic goodwill requires its organon or organically organised group instrument. And to a very considerable extent these have been growing all over the world in preparation for this very period of history in which we now find our place. During the last two centuries, most visibly in Europe and America and the British Commonwealth, but elsewhere as well, what are now called non-governmental organisations have been increasing their numbers. They are groups, some vast in membership and some small, through which the ordinary citizen can take action along the lines that interest him.

They touch every field of human activity. Some are selfish or at least intensely self-protective of special interests. But a very great number are motivated by goodwill and are charitable, creative and outgoing. These are like health-giving cells in the bodies of nations. And also, where they are international in scope, in the life exchange between nations.

Now, in relation to our special study, let us propose that it is possible to take this development a stage further —sharpening and intensifying the beneficial influence of such cellular organisations. There is an old magical catchphrase which reveals an obvious truism, namely that 'potency produces precipitation'. Where energy builds up in potency during the course of creative work, things happen, there is a break-through, a contact between the universes, an exchange between subjective and objective which allows the precipitation or concretisation of some inner plan.

Throughout history cultures have been formed and reformed by the intensive action of relatively small groups or cells. These cultures, when they have been anchored through some particular work, have then qualified and coloured the development of civilisation with their vibration. The energy of the Greek socratic thinkers focused through the writings of Plato is still influencing our civilisation today. Christ and his disciples provide an even more obvious example on the grand scale.

These culture-shocks, as they have been called, keep human society galvanised and on the move. In our own recent European history one can see them operating in a multitude of different ways: the philosophers and musicians of the German-speaking nations, the French school of impressionist painters, the Fabian group with the Webbs, Bernard Shaw and others in Britain. There are a mass of examples.

And, of course, the more humble citizen, whose quota of talent may not shine so brightly as history's giants, can also play a part. By joining his efforts with several of those whose minds and hearts vibrate in tune with his, their combined energy may cumulatively reach sufficient potency to produce some precipitation.

The witches of old had their covens. And some of their modern sisters defensively explain that this simply means 'a religious gathering'. Why should not the men and women of goodwill, who wish to work creative magic, have their organons? Each focused for action in the direction of their choice. Of course, they do not need to be called organons, that is simply a term we have employed to sum up the vision on which they can be founded. They can work under the label of action committee, unit of service, working party or what you will, or even use no title at all, if that is feasible. The important thing is that they exist and understand their function of galvanising human creativity in a beneficial and constructive way.

THE STRUCTURE OF THE ORGANONS

Many organisations, fired by goodwill, exist and make sterling contributions to society. However, for those who are embarking on new work and would like to experiment there is a definite structure for organons which has been discussed in an intriguing work on magic. This I pass on now for what it is worth, believing in fact that it can be practically useful in making action more pointed and potent, quite apart from any esoteric value which the structure may have.

It is suggested that a membership of nine is a particularly useful organic group structure. This is obviously practical in so far as it is not too large for management, particularly if members are geographically separate. On the other hand it is large enough to subdivide into three groups of three should special concentration on components of a project be necessary.

However, just as certain lodges and various legendary groups had a numerical make-up which carried a particular mystical significance, so it appears the organons of nine have a special occult value.

There is a clue in a book called *A Treatise on Cosmic Fire*, by A. A. Bailey. This work, incidentally, makes a deep analysis of black and white magic. The material is not all verifiable by present-day science, but it does make an intuitive appeal to many, and is accepted at least as a working hypothesis by many more.

In various parts of this book there is an examination of arcane knowledge about the human essence or soul, and in one place there is a written description of what one might call the direct organon or subtle instrument of the essential human ego or soul, through which it contacts the mental, emotional and physical parts of the personality that make up its outer apparatus. This instrument is like the causal body of theosophical doctrine or the lighted ovoid sometimes seen at the centre of the human aura by clairvoyants.

To quote exactly from the book, the description runs as follows:

For instance, the body of the Ego may be viewed in the following four ways:

As nine vibrations, emanating from a central point, which in its pulsation or radiations produces three major vibrations of great force pursuing a circular activity around the centre; the nine vibrations pursue a diagonal path until they reach the periphery of the egoic sphere of influence. At this point they swing round, thus forming the well-known spheroidal form of the causal body.

As nine petals of a lotus, radiating from a common centre, and hiding within themselves three central petals, which conceal a central point of fire. The radiations from the tip of each petal are those which cause the illusion of a spheroidal shape.

As nine spokes of a wheel, converging towards a central hub, which hides the central energy or dynamo of force—the generator of all the activity.

As nine types of energy which produce definite emanations from a threefold unit, again itself an outgoing from a central unit of force.

For all purposes, the second definition will be the one of the most use to us in our attempt to picture the constitution, nature, method of development and true evolution of the Ego, functioning in the causal body.

In another book, *A Treatise on the Seven Rays*, Volume II, the same author speaks about the desirability of forming groups of nine awakened people who have some capacity to hold the mind up to the light of the soul, who can blend the energy of their hearts together, and who are capable of some manner of creativity along humanitarian, artistic, literary, philosophic or scientific lines. And the instruction goes on to say that where such a goodwill group exists it can be absorbed into the divine circulatory flow of life and become a magical channel for grace and blessing.

From all of which it would appear that these organons of nine men and women of goodwill are intended to represent the structure of the essential causal vehicle of the human soul or ego, right here at a practical physical level. And as few amongst us are truly soul-infused personalities in our daily waking consciousness, we gain the protective potency to work magic safely and creatively by operating in this group formation.

Of course, it is not only in *A Treatise on Cosmic Fire* that the mystical significance of this structure of nine, the triple trinity, comes to the fore. One modern church organisation reportedly uses it in its administrative units. It also plays a significant role in myth.

And it is interesting to see that in this role the number nine represents a relating factor, something or other which joins and connects the transcendental and infinite with the finite and mundane, which is exactly what our goodwill organons are intended for.

There are nine muses who bring upliftment and inspiration to creative man. In Nordic legend, interpreted by Wagner's famous music dramas of *The Ring* cycle, there are nine Valkyrie, those daughters of the union between the King of the gods and the Earth Mother, who have the duty of leading the heroes from the battlefields of this world to Valhalla, the abode of gods.

This same basic concept is inherent in many versions of the ageless wisdom which state that there are nine particular steps in expansion of consciousness, nine major initiations or specific Copernican revolutions, through which the human being passes on his way from beasthood to godhood.

The ninth wave rises highest, as one old saying goes. And in their function of relating the highest and the lowest, the groups of nine are redemptive.

Hercules, when he met the monstrous nine-headed Hydra, whose heads re-grew as fast as he lopped them off, eventually subdued it by lifting it into the air and out of contact with the earth from which it drew its strength.

Louis Pauwels in Chapter 2 of his book *The Morning of the Magicians* (also known as *The Dawn of Magic*) mentions 'the legend of the nine unknown men' who act as guardians of the secrets of science. They communicate amongst themselves, according to the version of the story which he discusses, by means of a synthetic language, and each possesses a book constantly being rewritten, in which the hidden wisdom of each one's particular branch of knowledge is contained. Drawing his information from an earlier book by Talbot Mundy, Pauwels lists the nine departments of secret science as: Techniques of propaganda and psychology (one subject), physiology, microbiology, transmutation of metals, communication, gravitation, cosmogony, light and sociology.

An experiment in creative activity by an occultist who tried to form nine groups of nine people each, listed the fields for applied work as telepathic communication, trained observation, magnetic healing, education for the new age, political organisation, work in religion, scientific service, psychology, finance and economy (one subject). Volume I of *Discipleship in the New Age* by A. A. Bailey has an account of this particular effort.

For the darker side of magic, Shakespeare in his *Macbeth* has the famous witches conclude their enchantments with the following incantation:

> The weird sisters, hand in hand,
> Posters of the sea and land,
> Thus do go about, about:

Thrice to thine, and thrice to mine,
And thrice again, to make up nine:
Peace!—the charm's wound up.

The charm, however, does not have to wind up a dark one. The organons of nine creative men and women of goodwill can be harbingers of spiritual peace.

Right now, more than ever before, the ordinary citizen has a chance and a responsibility to help in administering the culture-shocks which will move society into the Aquarian age. If for no other reason than the fact that our public problems are so intense, we cannot avoid involvement. And if they are given on a wide scale by many groups operating through different activities these shocks may not be so shocking. The greater the depth and breadth of understanding, the less the change-over will seem to be a destructive sweeping away of the old, and the more it will become a harmonious adaptation and co-operative welcoming of the new.

In previous less disturbed eras which lacked our public communication medias a tremendous accumulative effort was required. Creative change was often hung up, waiting for an assembly of high-grade people to spearhead the movement. Today, with more people of goodwill understanding that their day of opportunity is now, we can move ahead more rapidly and more gracefully, if we want to.

THE GREAT MAGICIAN

Many instances of innovators whose effect was magical shine out of the pages of the history books. Just for a moment let us touch lightly on a very few examples of the fairly recent movements in the West that have contributed to the present opportunity. There is the work of people like Cosimo de Medici, who did much to finance the Italian renaissance. He was one of the first examples of an international banker in something like the modern sense. He was also a mystic and would retire to a monastic cell for retreats from his worldly work. There is the example set at the court of Margaret of Navarre where many Hellenic teachers and philosophers collected in France. Then there were the scholars and writers who assembled in England and were touched by the type of vision which Thomas More and Francis Bacon anchored in such works as *Utopia* and *The New Atlantis*, both of which visualised the defeat of ignorance. Later there appeared the American group round Washington, Jefferson and Franklin, who determined to work out Thomas Paine's ideas and found a nation on the Masonic ideal of being happy and communicating happiness.

It is relatively easy to send up culture, and all too easy to point to the defects of civilisation. Very frequently some original spark of inspiration is ill-conducted. Then some system it has galvanised becomes mechanical and turns into a cage instead of being the dwelling for free souls which was intended.

But true cultures are the product of much heart-searching on the part of great men. And some of the tangible treasures of civilisation now lie so thickly in our museums, where we can often look at them for free, that we almost take for granted the incredible creative magic that has precipitated these gifts on to the physical plane.

I believe that back behind culture and civilisation there is a great 'light of nature' which is designed to play its part in revealing 'the essence of things'. And in the service of this light, civilisation has had its messengers, its pathfinders and its avatars, just as races and religions have.

Science, for instance, is a branch of civilisation which is currently administering many culture-shocks. Look how, we respect its sages and praise the work of a Newton, a Harvey, a Galileo or an Einstein. The dedicated will and intuitive faith which impelled the Curies to render down those many tons of pitch-blend till they revealed radium is surely a form of discipleship to life itself. I do not think anyone would get the wrong idea if we said that science has had its saints.

At certain times men have acclaimed this light of nature which is behind the influence of civilisation as an aspect of the divine presence. The ancient Athenians, who birthed democracy, enshrined it in the form of Pallas Athene. Her wisdom was said to guide the city state. And in myths there are half-recollected images of old initiate kings and goddesses like Lilith whose worship guided sections of the old Atlantean culture. Entwined with the far-reaching influences of race and religion, yet playing a distinct part which can often overcome barriers set up by both these two, civilisation is frequently personified in some way. It is like the creative thread of some vast antahkarana or inner instrument which is being built by the whole human race. But while the radiation of its influence may be regarded as a something, its personifications are similarly a someone. We know so very little about superhuman forms of life, but it is quite possible that civilisation, throughout its many incarnations, is an entity.

There are mystical ageless wisdom-teachings which, in dealing with concepts of the triune expression of deity, the three-in-one idea to be found in both Eastern and Western religions, have pictured differently qualified agencies assisting the divine plan for human and planetary maturity. In doing this they are simply trying to point out channels to which Aquarian man can go with his pitcher, in order to help in circulating the waters of life.

One such agency has been called the Lord of Civilisation. An Eastern title is the Mahachohan, which simply means the great lord. It is he who works to relate the inner and the outer worlds, filling form with essence and using its magnetic radiation to call men forth to creativity. Coaxing them, drawing them, impelling them to come from the highways and byways, he inspires them to use every rightful charm of art, every artifact of science, every element of social justice to adapt their intelligence for growth and maturity.

Many accept the call of civilisation and are prepared to call themselves civilised, without regarding it as a narrow, confining label. For the arms of the Lord of Civilisation are wide and ready to embrace mankind whether he be agnostic, religious or non-believer.

And in this embrace men are lifted to where they may be better able to benefit from those great heart-melting experiences lived through by the various Buddhas and the Christ, on behalf of all.

What may lie beyond this point, in the future of the human race, we do not know. But, in the meantime, whatever exalted spirit may fulfil the office, the Lord of Civilisation works on through the channel provided by those who answer his appeal.

And this combined work of the servants of civilisation focuses what Bacon referred to as the intellectual light which is the crown and the consummation of creation, so that it reaches into the darkest corners of the human household. There it awakens men to a miraculous journey of exploration into self, into planet, into solar system, universe and God.

The Lord of Civilisation is master magician. And to be such he must be a lord of compassion as well.

4 *The Priesthood of Melchisedeck*

EXPLORERS

Once when I was in New York I visited the Roerich Museum. Here many pictures by the Russian painter and scenic designer Nicholas Roerich are on show. The museum guardian kindly took me through the gallery and commented on some of the work. Several pictures had for a subject the Altai Himalayan mountain range. One particular picture had in the foregound a plain and ascended in the background to a high and beautiful mountain.

The guardian told me the following story about the place which this picture represented. The mountain stood sentinel for a specially sacred area, and when going to it the local guides would take a traveller just so far. Then they would not go on. If questioned they would reply, 'If you cannot proceed by yourself, we have no right to take you. And if you can go on, you do not need us.'

This is the story of growth. It is also the story of faith. There comes a time when having made every wise and possible preparation, we must take a seeming leap in the dark. Before it comes there must be many occasions when we turn back again and again for assurance, when teachers, parents and friends must itch to push us out of some private nest, like a fledgling bird. And if we do not make that jump when we know interiorly that we should, then we can crystallise and literally become like the proverbial pillar of salt.

It is time humanity made such a jump. Inevitably in a conglomerate like the human race there will be individuals working through their lives in many states of experience. But a new 'high' in consciousness has to be reached by an influential portion of humanity if we are to make a creative digestion of the amount of life energy which is now our inheritance. And if one cares to register this life energy in no other way, the number of human units of energy now incarnate on the globe will do for a practical start.

It is probably indicative of our wavering on the brink of take-off that we often hear our troubles blamed on mediocre or indecisive leadership. This is foolishness. Our leaders are so often corporate projections of ourselves *en masse*.

Of course, totalitarianism can always find leadership, because it is a system which has thrown over the idea of balance. Duality, in the shape of one end or the other, is temporally supreme. And where extremes are the rule it is easy to enshrine a figurehead. But such dictators are an intoxicant which is temporally dominating part of the human body.

The tendency of humanity to throw up leadership images is most interesting. They cover a whole range from the pop idol to the spiritual avatar. Different cycles of time have produced different heroes and 'stars', and have employed many systems of selection. We appear to need these emblems of our own potential. Quite aside from those with appeal for special groups, there is always a good showing of public personalities: aristocrats, politicians, sportsmen, film- or song-stars. The more sophisticated our society, as for instance in the West, the more we seem to need these guides and crave the comfort of their presence. Who will emerge in the future? Perhaps astronauts stand a chance of being next in line. Except that these remarkable technicians show a very relaxed public image, which may indicate an under-the-surface shift in public values. Have we reached a place where we instinctively realise that all the symbols of social success are guides who can take us just so far?

There is a more subtle leadership which operates through the agency of humanity's civilising activities. It may emerge through the outstanding work of some remarkable individual, a Florence Nightingale, a Pope John or a Martin Luther King. Or on the other hand it may pervade our lives through the radiant influence of some working group.

While we cry for leadership, we forget to recognise the guidance that is available all the time. The essential livingness of work which has been anchored in this outer universe by the great of soul is all around us. There is a continuity of leadership that has in it no trace of dictatorial command. Its only lure is the loveliness of what is being offered.

THE DOOR IN THE WHEEL

So many mystical teachings have poetically spoken of the wheel of life that it has become one of those phrases we accept without thinking what it means. But most of us must have experienced the feeling of being stuck in the revolve of our own routines, whatever deeper significance we may eventually find in the words. When we accept some guidance that has emerged as an activity of soul, whether this comes forth from within ourselves or through the cultural service of others, and in consequence of it experience some degree of heart-melting, then we escape the wheel and find the door which is its pivot.

In terms of everyday life we may see this manifest as a change of heart, a shift in climate of opinion or some other subjective development in the individual or the group, which spurs creative activity.

I remember once visiting a small group of women who met from time to time in a converted mill. One entered the building across a little bridge. It had been built for its functional, rather than its symbolic value, though in the circumstances that too was present. Where the wheel had once turned there stood a door, and one passed over the mill stream to reach it. Inside, the women gathered in an upper room. The casement window looked out over the expanse of water feeding the mill stream to the woods beyond.

The meetings took the form of meditation and reflective discussion. Perhaps in times of repression and terror the group might have been suspect as some sort of conclave of white witches. But there was no outer form of ritual or special observance. A bowl gong sounded, and as its clear note focused inner attention, one could almost feel the quality of the peacefulness in the surrounding countryside. Tiny sounds, like the crackle of the open fire or one's own breathing, brought a calm which stilled even the chattering of the eternal monkey in one's mind. If anyone had asked me for a description of what was being done by the group, I would have said they were listening.

Passing from this refreshment of consciousness the group talked calmly together and when they had concluded their exchange the members went downstairs to a simple, home-cooked meal. Each of those taking part was playing an active part in social and community affairs. And the meetings in the upper room inspired them and their work.

Such groups have always existed, they have met in freedom and behind locked doors. They have sometimes included well-known people, but more often their membership was anonymous from the public point of view. They are what we have called organons, functioning on behalf of the culture of their time and place. They are open, thoughtful, undogmatic, observant and compassionate. And they offer the gift of hope and good seeds for the future.

But, of course, in relating the invisible with the seen there is much paradox. Just when one believes one has achieved a point of inner attention, one may in fact be most inattentive. One can trick oneself with beliefs about one's stance, instead of just getting on with it. I recall once having experienced a fine sense of buoyancy in consciousness during meditation. I proceeded into the kitchen to prepare breakfast, a stream of enchanting ideas exhilarating my mind. I only came to earth with a splash when I discovered myself attempting to boil an egg by putting it into a filled coffee cup.

THE LOTUS

A group channel is useful for maintaining balance. The different qualities provided by the various members of a working party help to stabilise each other. In moments of distraction and difficulty the co-workers can strengthen each other's vision. This is the outer and obvious strength of an organon.

But if we accept the hint given in *A Treatise on Cosmic Fire*, the groups of nine represent those subtle energies which provide a bridge between tangible man and that part of him which dwells within the other, unseen universe.

Let us, if only as a stimulating imaginative exercise, take the imagery of a lotus as suggested. Each man's spiritual qualities are represented by latent energies which as they unfold and manifest in response to the development of his consciousness, appear inwardly as the petals of an illuminated lotus, a lotus which really does represent the truth as the lotus is supposed to do, because it reveals what a man essentially is at the heart of his being. A lotus form which is a vehicle for his soul.

These energies when still dormant are like the tight knot of a closed bud. They unfold petal by petal as life experience removes our crusts and allows what Browning called the imprisoned splendour to emerge.

The esoteric teachings maintain that lifetime by lifetime the lotuses gradually flower. The outer three petals are influenced by knowledge and the growth of intelligence. The middle three unfurl as the experience of love touches us in ever more profound ways. And the final three which veil the central core of energy—referred to in some

Eastern spiritual literature as the jewel in the lotus—are called the petals of sacrifice. These come alive as we learn to relate consciously and intentionally with that which is greater than ourselves, and as we come to understand how we may live life more abundantly by giving ourselves up to it.

In forming group replicas of the lotuses, which we have called organons, the personnel of the groups represent the energy of the petals. Working together they are a ritual for the conveyance of soul energy.

That agency which brings the touch of the other universe to the central core of the lotus, whether that core be within a human being or a working group of men of goodwill, is known to the ageless wisdom schools as the solar angel. It is the life-giving agency of which the sun is the spiritual emblem. It is man's inner guardian whose silent will works behind the scenes. It is the angelic dweller in a kingdom not of this world or universe. It represents and channels what St. Paul called 'Christ in us, the hope of glory'.

LORDS OF COMPASSION

Those strange words, glory, joy, harmony, pervade the world's scriptures. Again and again they try to draw man's sight to the frontiers of the other universe. Mystics talk of grace and metaphysicians of universal harmony. The Upanishads speak of the joy from which all creatures are born. And in St. John's gospel Christ tells us of the Father's glory which was before the worlds were made. And this to a world that knows hell on earth. All indicating that there is a quality, not quite discernible to the senses, which man can touch with his intuitive consciousness and which is capable of transforming outer conditions.

Man's prevailing interest in magic is the measure of his hope that doors can be opened through which this glory, harmony or joy may pervade our beleaguered world.

We will take a key statement from H. P. Blavatsky's writings, simply because we have used a statement of hers to find a title. The same thing has been said many times: 'Compassion is no attribute, it is the law of laws; Alaya's Self. Eternal Harmony. The law of everlasting right, and fitness of all things. The law of love eternal.' Compassion summarises the opening of the lotus through sacrifice, love and true intelligence. It invokes the presence of the solar angel who is the harbinger of harmony.

Toynbee's statement about human concern for the welfare of all, the agencies of the United Nations organistion, certain governments and many charitable groups, the new public recognition of the value of ecology and its attendant caring sciences, all these take on a deep significance in so far as they are indications of the birth of a compassionate world society.

In a remarkable book, *The Woman Who Could Not Die*, the authoress Yulia de Beausabre describes a period in her life when she was imprisoned by a totalitarian regime. Part of this experience involved many months of solitary confinement, at the end of which her cell was shared only by mad or abnormal people. She kept herself going by a variety of subjective exercises. She has written out the revelation of one of her meditations in the following words:

Out of the confines of eternity I flow to man as light. From man I flow to man as warmth. When the great sun rises in the heart of man, I flow back to the limits of eternity as love. I am the pivot of the human world. I am security. My breath is Peace. Seek in the miracle of warmth flowing from harrowed man to harrowed man. Seek and you will find me.

Joel S. Goldsmith, the American mystic, spoke in some of his talks about 'Melchisedeck—Christ—the man who was never born and who will never die'. The ancient of days is that spirit of which we are all part, and of which men can become priests and servers. Compassion makes conscious relationship within the empire of Melchisedeck a possibility. It is also the light by which we can travel through the dark when the guides seem to have departed.

Of course, as we know, the guides are not far from us. Much of the tangible work of great souls remains in the world as a channel for their influence. And also as a reminder that there are those who have touched those deep currents of energy where the lotus unfolds and compassion is born on the fiery wings of the solar angels.

If the message through which compassion comes to us is very great, we may allow myopic human vision to quarrel on points of interpretation. But is it not in the nature of those of great vision, who have stood before us like archetypes, that they feed many types of men? Each of us reacts according to the portion of their message we are able to digest, just as many will respond to a fine painting or exciting music, but not all in the same way. This only proves the avatar's capacity to nourish all sorts of men in many states and conditions of life. And in fact the deeper the nourisher has gone in his own transforming digestion of life's energy, the wider will be his transmitting capacity. This is particularly true of great lights like Christ and Buddha, regardless of what we may feel about them personally.

Carl Jung always recommended wrestling with archetypes when we made contact with them. If we did not do this they absorbed us, he maintained. If this happens we are no longer such a responsible servant as if we had stood strong beside them, making use of all our faculties. One can see it happen in a simple way, so easily, where well-meaning people have become part of the structure of some organisation which has lost the original spirit that founded it and is maintained by a thought-form. In a psychic sense one sees it occur where fanaticism and obsession have taken over. The archetype is not to blame, for it simply is what it is. We, for the time being, have been unable to digest and transform the archetypal energy in terms of our own environment. It is a bit like Jacob wrestling with the angel. The quality we succeed in touching we had better make our own or let it pass.

Those great ones who have made themselves Lords of compassion by educating themselves to carry its quality, are like a chain of dynamos. And they fire other hearts and minds with their goodwill. This is a leadership which speaks to man's essence, ignites man's heart through the solar angel, and leaves him free to grow with the unfoldment of the lotus. Which, as we have described, takes place inwardly at a subtle level and also can be accelerated through an outward replica formed for service.

There may well be awakened consciousnesses who are as far ahead of us in outlook as the average educated, well-nourished women and men of goodwill seem to be from the starved, misery-loaded multitudes in the streets of say Calcutta's shanty town.

But such a seeming lead, where it remains compassionate, is not that of superman or big brother. It must be that of the concerned and caring companion, who wants to find a way through, who wants to open the path of relationship so that good may result, who wants to let the harmonies he has known touch other lives, who works ceaselessly for a creative world society, and awaits response.

Throughout, goodwill must bridge the gaps. This often means making the right spiritual compromise, or rendering to each level the things of that level, though always with the larger end in sight, until such time as a greater dynamic energy can lift and transform a lesser one. To put this in plain terms we will take a precise and definite example.

Say a world leader states that the ideal way to use man's sexual function is through the employment of rhythmical control. If man understands and lets his energy respond to the great law of cycles, all will be well. This is the vision; the serpent-standard held up in a wilderness seething with vipers. But following on this comes a recognition of events taking place in time and space. Of millions and millions of spawning people who do not see this vision, who do not understand any cycle much beyond the coming of light and dark and birth and death, and who only wait for sustenance. Then, for compassion's sake, leadership can also say, teach hygiene, employ mechanical aids which intelligence has provided, alleviate suffering so that the people can begin to hear something beyond their own cries.

THE LUNAR LORDS

Colin Wilson, the British writer who first made his mark with his book *The Outsider*, has published a fantasy novel called *The Mind Parasites*. In this tale he has drawn on a concept which is not uncommon among esoteric groups. In some circles the mind parasites of the story are referred to as the lunar lords.

Broadly speaking these are the multitude of forces in man which, left each to go his own way, will war amongst themselves. They can then convert into the self-destructive forces which man is obviously capable of unleashing, whether in the shape of direct or indirect inhumanity to fellow-man, or in the form of the furies within ourselves which we sometimes let tear us asunder; the lunar lords are clever at disguise.

In one of the Belgian philosopher Maurice Maeterlinck's plays about Tytyl, the woodcutter's son who is the hero of his famous story of the Bluebird of Happiness, the boy is given a magic cap. In the forefront of this cap is a diamond; when he turns it he will see things as they are. At one point in his adventures when he is undecided about the next best thing to do he turns the diamond and finds himself surrounded by a great crowd of different-sized versions of himself. He is being tugged and pulled in so many different directions that he nearly comes apart. But fortunately he has control of the diamond which temporally gave form to these different-shaped selves.

The whole point about the lunar lords is that they are not powers in themselves, however horrendous they may seem to be. They remain *doppel-gängers* which we can absorb. They are, as their name implies, satellites who react according to where we place our centre of gravity.

We hold the jewel at the centre of the lotus within us, like the diamond in Tytyl's cap. Beyond the jewel stands the soul or solar angel, ready, according to the measure in which we can release it into this world, to realign the negative forces so that they become useful parts of the outworking of universal harmony.

Whether in ourselves or in others we should consider the lunar influences in an impersonal way. Like duality they perform at their level according to prevailing influence. They are not the essential human being, but partially awoken elements of his living apparatus.

It is part of magic, whether it comes in ancient guise or in the garment of modern psychology, to tame and harness these elemental currents which are in us all. And we begin this training as soon as we recognise for ourselves where our true substance and centre are.

In the first chapter, where we spoke of white and black magic, we said that a more appropriate naming was possible. Solar and lunar magic would certainly serve as well as white and black.

LUNAR CYCLES

Tied in with the symbolism of the solar angel evaporating the negative influence of the lunar lords is the practical use that can be made of the lunar cycles in relation to meditation. The cycles of new moon and full moon have been given responsibility for a great deal in the course of human history, and their effect on vegetable growth and on the tides of the sea is accepted generally. What still remains wide open to research is the kind of effect they have in relation to consciousness or at least on the parts of human mechanism through which consciousness chiefly operates.

To state the obvious, at the time of full moon we receive the maximum available quantity of life-imparting energy from the sun. The moon, quite aside from the fact that it is not getting in the way of the sunlight as is the case at the time of the dark of the moon, is around the other side of the world fulfilling, to some extent, the function of a reflector. Again one should stress that the negative element is not necessarily harmful of itself. Like Kundry it fulfils its function malevolently or benevolently, according to where it is placed. The key is in the type of relationship we set up.

Many occultists believe that there is a subtle psychic and spiritual equivalent of the outer sunlight and its high tides. They make use of the full-moon period as a high point in their group meditation work, somewhat as though it were a peak experience within the all-inclusive meditation rhythm of Melchisedeck.

The days immediately prior to the full-moon period are taken as a time of preparation and orientation towards that which is transcendental and sublime. The actual day of the full moon is marked by a quiet, inner, attentive receptivity, while the following day or so there is a deliberate return from the mountain peak, as it were. Attention is focused once more on outer projects and services with the idea of distributing and passing on whatever inspiration and refreshment may have been registered. Whether this is considered to be a symbolic piece of ritual or an actual channelling of energy, its value as a mental exercise is clear.

It fulfils the gathering in and giving out motion of

breath itself, not forgetting, of course, the fractional pause or interlude between the inward and outward motion. It is in the interlude that things happen, chemical interchange takes place in breathing or shift in consciousness takes place in meditation. This is all part of the mechanics of magic.

There is naturally a lower interlude as well, between the breathing out and the breathing in again. This can be seen in the totality of the moon cycle. Just as the full-moon period can be one of invocation towards the unseen universe and that which it stands for, so the new-moon period can be one of evocation of its outer correspondence, a time of out-working, earthing and anchoring. The successful working of this cycle is one way of bringing 'the Above and the Below . . . together' in order that they may act in harmony. At the high point we build potency, at the deep point we have opportunity to precipitate.

And, of course, rhythm is the clue to a constructive handling of the elemental lunar forces in ourselves. Sometimes an event precipitates which offers distinct inner messages as well as a number of more obvious outer values, and both can be of practical significance. Is the fact that man has now set his foot upon the moon symbolic of the fact that the wise handling of lunar forces, within our society, is within our collective grasp? Our resources are sufficient, our intelligence has the capability, we must summon our compassionate goodwill.

THE RIDER ON THE WHITE HORSE

When considering the intangible we can approach it

through so many different forms of thought. And all of them veil it as much as they reveal it.

Another ancient thought-form associated with magic which we should try and pierce is the idea of the lords of karma, those legendary beings who are considered to have charge of the rules of cause and effect. Their activity is tangled up with all manner of beliefs about fate, predestination and free-will. They are a bit like the four genii which, Arabian myth maintained, held up the corners of the earth.

In any event they represent the rule of human law and the sway of the four elements. Here the ancient symbol of the square is being made to represent humanity once again. And in their darkest aspect these lords of karma are seen as the four terrible horsemen of the Apocalypse, spreading their pestilence, famine, war and hatred. But in less gruesome form they are just the inevitable fruitage of the seeds of action. Recent arcane teaching names them as Action, which is what the word 'karma' means anyway, Relationship, Pain and Return.

If we analyse these titles and meditate on what they really represent we will quickly see that they are only agencies for life and consciousness. Action entwines the two. Relationships, through which we communicate with one and other and the universe around, can be made joyful or unhappy. Pain can be a medical warning, a chastening tutor or the vehicle for human cruelty. And Return, a motion of the wheel of life when its true nature is understood, is perhaps the most deeply compassionate potential of all, for it brings us back, to confront opportunities, challenges and problems, again and again and again, giving us the inestimable gift of another try.

How often do we inwardly cry out, like a child in a game, for another chance. The contention of the ageless wisdom is that our present span of consciousness is so circumspect and curtailed that we do not recognise that merciful providence does in fact give us another go in the shape of rebirth.

The Association for Research and Enlightenemnt, founded in America as a result of the work and writings of Edgar Cayce, is one present-day organisation which is investigating this avenue of man's experience.

But to continue: when we settle in to a consideration of the four horsemen who carry the influence of human cause and effect, another symbolic horseman comes riding into consciousness from the direction of the other universe. If the four horsemen represent the world as we know it and all its ways, then the rider on the white horse represents that which surmounts and absorbs their influence.

It is easy to see that this rider is the classic hero figure of mythology. St. George confronting the dragon is an obvious example. Also, let us not forget, Christ entering Jerusalem on an ass.

In one occult invocation, which, like O'Casey's great cry in *Juno and the Paycock*—'Oh, blessed heart of Jesus; take away our hearts of stone and give us hearts of flesh' —appeals for compassion and liberation, this figure is referred to as 'the rider from the secret place'.

> Let the Lords of Liberation issue forth.
> Let Them bring succour to the sons of men.
> Let the Rider from the Secret Place come forth.
> And coming, save.
> Come forth, O Mighty One.

The classics of spiritual literature are, of course, peppered with some sort of reference to a secret or mysterious place which cannot be described in earthly terms. The phrase from the psalms, 'the secret place of the most high', is in almost constant use among modern metaphysical churches.

Most sets of belief have something to say about a holy city. The idea of Shamballa, Shangri-la, the true Jerusalem, the mighty Valhalla, are all similar as a place of peace and an abode of the enlightened. This concept, whether it is thought of as a location or a state of consciousness, seems to represent an outpost of the other universe. Some people even maintain that that is where existences more exalted than our own, from elsewhere in our universe, send their embassies. The whole subject is hemmed around with a multitude of thought-forms and interpretations.

If we do nothing else now, we can at least be thankful for the hope enshrined in the concept and consider it as the poetic courts of heaven from which the white horse has come forth again and again, bearing those who are committed to the work of succouring and salvaging the world, and whose loving presence has the capacity to short-circuit the rule of earthly karma and bring the grace and blessing of compassionate harmony.

The white horse is spiritual light and energy, the radiance of the solar angel, beaming forth from the unseen universe. And this energy carries its passenger in the shape of a human consciousness into adventure and service.

At the time of the investiture service at Caernarvon Castle, when Prince Charles took on the title Prince of

Wales, he gave an interview on television. In the course of an easy, unpretentious discussion he mentioned his family motto 'I serve'. I do not recollect his exact words but he said something to the effect that while it might not appear to mean very much, he would be thinking of it at the time of the ceremony, even if no one else was.

We have already mentioned the spiritual effect of the dedication to service in relation to Kundry, and at this point it is worth repeating what we have written elsewhere.* In a book called *The Destiny of the Nations* by A. A. Bailey it is stated that the esoteric motto of Great Britain, and presumably, though this is not made clear, of its Commonwealth Association, is the same as that of the royal family. However, there need be no sense of proprietary right about this because in an ancient occult text the same battle-cry, 'I serve', is given as the basic keynote of the West. The old writing goes as follows:

> From out the East, bring a light divine, the word comes swinging round the square: Love all.
> From out the West, the answer is flung back: I serve.

The keynote of the West is a counterpart to the keynote of the East. It is a practical response to the message of compassion.

The East, being the region where the sun arises, gives birth to the foundational spiritual message of love, compassion and harmony. The word or note of the message swings round humanity's four-square city. In the West, the place to which the sun must travel and to which its light inevitably reaches, love is worked out visibly

* *The Mystical Ladder.*

through service. And so the invisible and intangible comes to be seen by all.

Duality is often personified by the East and the West, which Kipling maintained would never meet. But when the influence of the other universe comes into play they complement each other. And we can see the possibility of the harmonious correspondence between East and West, love and service, united by Christ, heir and representative of Melchisedeck, the ancient of days who was not born and cannot die and whose glory was with God before the worlds were made, finding expression through the creature man.

At a recent convention the American mystic Walter Starcke, who wrote *The Ultimate Revolution*, made the simple statement that 'in the priesthood of all mankind there is no one who cannot at some time give help to another'. Mankind is intended as the network that can relay the harmonising and rejuvenating energy of goodwill through the world and maybe beyond. The other universe stands in its magnificence. The riders, though often unseen, travel ceaselessly. Nothing remains but that we open our consciousness to the beneficent influences that are available and join together, as de Chardin would say, in building the earth.

As we turn to the unseen universe we honour God the father of all. As we return to the environment around us we honour God the mother of the world. The activity of the Lords of compassion and the antahkarana bridge of civilisation relate the two aspects of the holy union. Are the human children who issue from that union yet capable of acknowledging it?

In wondering again for what purpose the universes

came to being, and in trying to formulate one's own Parsifal question of the moment, I find I want to sum up what this chapter has tried to say. In casting round how I can do this, Christ's great words of comfort and encouragement come to mind. They can be our final seed for reflection:

> Fear not, little flock, it is the Father's good pleasure to give you the kingdom.
>
> Luke 12.32

5 *The Magician*

(From an old proclamation, quoted in *A Treatise on White Magic* by A. A. Bailey)

Let the magician stand within the great world sea. Let him immerse himself in water and there let him stand his ground. Let him look down into the watery depths. Nothing is seen in form correct. Nothing appears but water. Beneath his feet it moves, around him, and above his head. He cannot speak; he cannot see. Truth disappears in water.

Let the magician stand within the stream. Around him water flows. His feet stand firm on land and rock, but all the forms he sees are lost in the grey immensity of mist. The water is around his neck, but, feet on rock and head in air, he maketh progress. All is distortion still. He knows he stands, but where to go and how to go he knows not, nor understands. He sounds the words of magic, but muffled, dim and lost, the mist returns them to him, and no true note sounds forth. Around him are the many sounds of many forms, which swallow up his sound.

Let the magician stand in watery mist, free of the running stream. Some outlines dim appear. He sees a little distance on the Path. Flickers of light break through the clouds of mist and fog. He hears his voice; its note is clearer and more true. The forms of other pilgrims can be seen. Behind him is the sea. Beneath his feet is seen the stream. Around him mist and fog. Above his head no sky is seen nor sun.

Let the magician stand on higher ground, but in the rain. The drops pour down upon him; the thunder breaks; the lightning flashes in the sky. But as the rain pours down, it dissipates the mist, it washes clean the form and clears the atmosphere.

Thus forms are seen and sounds are heard, though dim as yet, for loud the thunder roars and heavy is the sound of falling rain. But now the sky is seen; the sun breaks forth and in between the drifting clouds, expanses of the blue of heaven cheer the tired eyes of the disciple.

Let the magician stand upon the mountain top. Beneath him in the valleys and the plains, water and streams and clouds are seen. Above him is the blue of heaven, the radiance of the rising sun, the pureness of the mountain air. Each sound is clear. The silence speaks with sound.

Let the magician stand within the sun, looking from thence upon the ball of earth. From that high point of peace serene let him sound forth the words that will create the forms, build worlds and universes and give his life to that which he has made. Let him project the forms created on the mountain top in such a way that they can cleave the clouds which circle round the ball of earth, and carry light and power. These shall dispel the veil of forms which hide the true abode of earth from the eye of the beholder.

Appendix: The Organons

This book is a rough-cut on a theme. It is four years since the plan for it arrived in my mind, somewhat inconveniently just as a plane in which I was travelling was about to land. It is three years ago that it was written and since then concepts have been developed, ideas clarified and sections re-drafted. This is not a fisherman's story about the salmon which one's small-fry offering could have been. It is said to emphasise that this whole area of study can never be static. For this reason this appendix containing background material on the building of Organons is offered to those who have found *The Other Universe* a spur to action.

The following compilation is drawn from the writings of Alice Bailey and Djwhal Khul. Some of the material is taken from general remarks about new age groups. Elsewhere it is drawn from information about a particular attempt Djwhal Khul initiated to form seed groups of nine with some of his own co-workers. This material has been slightly edited to give it general relevance, but the references are included so that any reader can look up the passages in the context of the published work if he should wish to.

The operational structure offered by such groups of nine can be adapted by anyone wishing to experiment in group work. The Human Development Trust is one organisation which is assisting a small number of autonomous groups to form on this basis. It does not run the groups, but does what it can to stimulate and encourage volunteers who are willing to convene useful group activities.

In the following extracts there are a number of references to 'inner groups' which generate the impulse on which objective working groups swing into action. There is no need to think of these inner groups in any too mysterious way; if one considers the sort of automatic subjective grouping that occurs between people with similar professional interests one will be on the right lines. In such cases people may not know each other as individuals but they are held together by the wavelength of their work and while their personal techniques and peculiarities may vary they share a certain subjective community of consciousness.

It is for similar communities of consciousness which are concerned with building a new world civilisation that the Organons can, as the meaning of their name implies, become 'instruments of group awareness'.

THE EXPERIMENTAL NATURE OF THE GROUPS

This experiment has a fourfold objective:

1. To found or start focal points in the human family through which certain energies can flow out into the entire race of men. These energies are ten in number. (Editorial note: Under the Chapter on The Lord of Civilisation on page 84 nine different types of work were mentioned; these represent, with an additional synthesising activity, channels for ten essential qualified energies.)
2. To inaugurate certain new techniques in work and in modes of communication. Note that in these last three

words the whole story is summed up. . . .

3. To externalise an inner existing condition. It must be realised that these groups are not a cause but an effect. They may themselves have an initiatory effect as they work upon the physical plane, but they are the product of inner activity and of subjective aggregations of force which must perforce become objective. The work of the group members is to keep, as a group, in close rapport with the inner groups, which form, nevertheless, one large, active group. This central group force will then pour through the groups to the extent the group members, as a group:

a. Keep *en rapport* with the inner sources of power,
b. Never lose sight of the group objective, whatever that objective may be,
c. Cultivate a dual capacity to apply the laws of the soul to the individual life, and the laws of the group to the group life,
d. Use all forces which may flow into the group in service, and learn, therefore, to register that force and use it correctly.

Would the following sequence of statements convey anything to your minds in this connection? They are statements of fact and not in the least symbolic in their terminology, except in so far as all words are inadequate symbols of inner truths.

Each group has its inner counterpart.

This inner counterpart is a complete whole. The outer result is only partial.

These inner groups, forming one group, are each of them expressive of, or governed by, certain laws, embodying the controlling factors in group work. A law is only an expression or manifestation of force, applied under the power of thought by a thinker or group of thinkers.

These inner groups, embodying differing types of force, and working synthetically to express certain laws, are an effort to bring in new and different conditions, and hence produce a new civilisation.

This is the new age that the Aquarian period will see consummated. The outer groups are a tentative and experimental effort to see how far humanity is ready for such an endeavour.

4. To manifest certain types of energy which will produce cohesion, or at-one-ment, upon earth. The present distraught condition in the world, the international impasse, the religious dissatisfaction, the economic and social upheaval of the past few decades, are all the result of energies that are so potent—owing to their immense momentum—that they can only be brought into rhythmic activity by the imposition of stronger and more definitely directed energies.

From: *A Treatise on the Seven Rays*, Volume II, pages 188–94.

NEW AGE GROUPS

New groups are appearing everywhere all over the world. The groups upon the outer plane, with their diversity of names and stated aims, are not connected with the inner group which is sponsoring or 'projecting' the new groups. However, a definite, even if nebulous, connection becomes possible where there are three members of the new group of world servers found in any one exoteric group; it then becomes 'linked by a triple thread of golden light' to the new group of world servers, and can in some measure be used. This great and spiritual grouping of servers is, on the physical plane, only very loosely linked. On the astral plane the linking is stronger and is based upon love of humanity; on the mental plane the major linking takes place from the angle of the three worlds as a whole. Certain developments must have taken place in the individual before he can consciously become a functioning member of the new group of world servers.

(Editorial note: The phrase 'the new group of world servers' has been used to describe that subjectively synthesised group of souls whose broad objective is the service of humanity—in its essential nature. This inner grouping is controlled by no earth-bound organisation and is not the product of any one particular school of thought. Broadly speaking, some of its goals have been visioned as: 'The clarifying of the international situation, the raising of human consciousness, and the growth and development of the group idea.')

1. He must have the heart centre awakened, and be so outgoing in his 'behaviour' that the heart is rapidly linked up with the heart centres of at least eight other people. Groups of nine awakened aspirants can then be occultly absorbed in the heart centre of the planetary Logos. Through it, His life can flow and the group members can contribute their quota of energy to the life influences circulating throughout His body. The above piece of information is only of interest to those who are spiritually awakened, and will mean little or nothing to those who are asleep.

2. The head centre must also be in process of awakening,

and the ability to 'hold the mind steady in the light' must be somewhat developed.

3. Some forms of creative activity must likewise be found and the server must be active along some humanitarian, artistic, literary, philosophic or scientific lines.

From: *A Treatise on the Seven Rays*, Vol. II, pages 196–8.

AN INNER PATTERN FOR THE NINE-FOLD STRUCTURE

H.P.B. speaks in *The Secret Doctrine* of the 'three periodical vehicles', referring to the Monad, the Soul and the Personality, which involve the nine aspects of divinity which connote the nine major initiations and those divine characteristics through which the three major aspects of divinity reflect themselves. In this connection, it is well known to students that the Monad expresses itself through the Spiritual Triad, the Soul through the three aspects of the Egoic Lotus, and the Personality through the three mechanical vehicles. It will be obvious to you surely that these three periodical vehicles are under the influence or impression of the three major planetary centres. (Editorial note: The Secret Place, Hierarchy and Humanity.) I do not feel it to be necessary to enlarge upon this basic relation; it is that which integrates the human soul into the vast general whole and makes the individual an intrinsic part of the sum total.

From: *Telepathy and the Etheric Vehicle*, page 134.

The material taken from *A Treatise on Cosmic Fire* on the nature of the body of the Ego, is also relevant. It is given in Chapter 3 under the section on the structure of the organons.

ONE POSSIBLE WORK FORMULA FOR GROUP USE

Three things are of great importance and constitute your individual responsibility:

1. Facility of rapport. As members of a group, it is essential that you cultivate two aspects of the 'art of rapport' which is based, eternally, on loving attraction.
    a. Rapport or contact with the soul through a cultivated alignment and correct meditation.
    b. Rapport or contact with your group brothers; this lays the foundation for constructive, united work.

2. Impersonality. Is there aught more that I can say on this theme? You must learn to view what is said or suggested by any group brother with a complete and carefully developed 'divine indifference'. Note the use of the word 'divine', for it holds the clue to the needed attitude. It is a different thing to the indifference of not caring, or the indifference of a psychologically developed 'way of escape' from that which is not pleasant; nor is it the indifference of superiority. It is the indifference which accepts all that is offered, uses what is serviceable, learns what can be learnt but is not held back by personality reactions. It is the normal attitude of the soul or self to the not-self. It is the negation of prejudice, of all narrow pre-conceived ideas, of all personality tradition, influence or background. It is the process of detachment from 'the world, the flesh and the devil' of which 'The New Testament' speaks.

3. Love. Love is that inclusive, non-critical, magnetic comprehension and attitude which (in group work) preserves the group integrity, fosters the group rhythm and permits no secondary personality happenings or

attitudes to mar the group work.

Contact, impersonality and love—these three constitute the individual objectives which I set before each and all of you.

The group requirements which must be met and preserved by the groups, as groups, are as follows:

1. Group integrity. This grows out of right integration and refers to the delicate balance which must be preserved amongst the members of a group. This is of such a nature that there emerges eventually a group steadiness and a group freedom from 'oscillation' which will permit of uninterrupted group work and interplay. It will come if each of the group members will simply mind his own business and permit of uninterrupted group work and interplay. It will come if each of the group members will simply mind his own business and permit his group brothers to mind theirs; it will come if you keep your personality affairs, your private concerns and troubles, out of the group life; it will come if you refrain from discussion of each other and of each other's affairs and attitudes. This is of supreme importance at this stage of the group work; it will mean—if you can achieve success in this—that you will be able to keep your minds clear of all lesser things which concern the personality life. This means that your minds will be free, therefore, for group work.

2. Fusion. By this I mean the ability of the group to work as a unit. This is dependent upon the achieving of right individual attitudes and (when working) the attainment of the capacity to lose sight of everything except the work to be done and a deeply sensed love of your brothers.

3. Understanding. I use this work in reference to your comprehension of the work to be undertaken. I do not use the word in reference to your attitude to yourself or to your group brothers. It means that each group works wisely and understandingly at its own appointed task, knowing that it contributes to a greater wholeness.

Integrity, fusion and understanding—this is the order of the work and the sequence of development. All groups, working in the outer world in relation to this concept of group activity, will follow certain initial and final stages in their work and these will be uniform for all the groups, no matter what their specific and individual group work may be. Thus there will be brought about an inter-group relation and a consequent strengthening of the individual groups.

Let me outline the stages to be followed:

Stage One

Alignment. Soul contact. Spiritual poise. Poise is the steady holding of the achieved soul contact.

a. Then, the conscious relinquishing of personality reactions.
b. Next, the recognition of the fact of love as an expression of that soul contact—expressed through the medium of the personality.
c. Finally, the imaginative fusion of the egoic and personality rays.

This constitutes the vertical stage.

Stage Two

The above is followed by group integration and group fusion, carried forward consciously.

a. By bringing each group member into conscious rapport through naming and loving.
b. By seeing all the group members as a circle of living points of light along with yourself in the circle, but not at the centre of the circle.
c. By imagining all these points of light as fusing and blending to make a radiant sun, with rays of light going out towards the four corners of the earth.

This constitutes the horizontal stage.

Stage Three

There follows next a careful consideration of group purpose. (Editorial note: At this point the specialised work tasks taken up by any particular group are brought into dynamic focus.)

Stages 1 and 2 should be rapidly effective and almost instantaneous in their results, after three months' careful work has been done. I request that you give careful, patient attention to them so that they develop eventually into stable habits and so give you no trouble and further difficulty. The initial stages in this type of work are of paramount importance.

Stage Four

Having finished the special group work under Stage 3, the members of each group will then endeavour to link up with the other groups in the same manner in which they linked up with the members of their own group. In this case, however, the members will not concern themselves with the personnel of any of the groups, including their own, but only—as a group—link their group with the other groups. Thus the concepts of illusion and of separateness, and the realisation of fusion will assume correct proportions in your minds.

a. Next, as a group, say an Invocation. (An example follows.)
b. Then sound the Sacred Word, the OM, three times.
c. Close with the prayer of the personality to the soul:
   'May the words of my mouth and the meditation of my heart be always acceptable unto thy sight, Oh, Soul, my Lord and my Redeemer.'

From: *Discipleship in the New Age*, Volume I, pages 59–62.

AN INVOCATION OF THE DIVINE PLAN

From the point of light within the mind of God
Let light stream forth into the minds of men.
Let light descend on earth.
From the point of love within the heart of God
Let love stream forth into the hearts of men.
May Christ return to earth.
From the centre where the will of God is known
Let purpose guide the little wills of men,
The purpose which the masters know and serve.
From the centre which we call the race of men
Let the plan of love and light work out
And may it seal the door where evil dwells.
Let light and love and power restore the plan on earth.

From: *The Reappearance of the Christ.*

A WORD AT THE END FOR REFLECTION

May I in all earnest offer to you the paradoxical injunction to work with utter earnestness, and yet at the same time to refuse to work with such earnestness, and not to take yourself so earnestly? Those who stand on the inner side and study the work of the world aspirants today see an almost pitiful distress of individual deficiency, a sustained and strenuous effort on their part to 'make themselves what they ought to be', and yet at the same time a distressing lack of proportion, and no sense of humour whatsoever. I urge upon you to cultivate both these qualities. Do not take yourself so seriously, and you will find that you will release yourself for freer and more potent work. Take the plan seriously and the call to serve, but waste not time in constant self-analysis.

Therefore the immediate goal for all aspiring servers at this time can be seen to be as follows:

1. An achievement of clarity of thought as to their own personal and immediate problems and primarily the problem as to their objective in service. This is to be done through meditation.
2. The development of sensitivity to the new impulses which are flooding the world at this time. This is to be brought about by loving all men more and through love and understanding contact them with greater facility. Love reveals.
3. The rendering of service with complete impersonality. This is done by eliminating personal ambition and love of power.
4. The refusal to pay attention to public opinion or to failure. This is done by the application of strict attention to the voice of the soul, and by an endeavour to dwell ever in the Secret Place of the Most High.

From: *A Treatise on White Magic*, pages 635–6.

Bibliography

Books, plays and operas quoted or mentioned in the text

The Golden Bough, James Fraser
Back to Methuselah, Bernard Shaw
The Perennial Philosophy, Aldous Huxley
Breakthrough to Creativity, Shafica Karagulla, M.D.
Psychosynthesis: A Manual of Principles and Techniques, Roberto Assagioli, M.D.
Freedom from the Known, J. Krishnamurti
A Sleep of Prisoners, Christopher Fry
The Secret Doctrine and *Isis Unveiled*, H. P. Blavatsky
The Hymn of the Universe, P. Teilhard de Chardin
A Midsummer Night's Dream and *Macbeth*, W. Shakespeare
Leaves of Grass, Walt Whitman
The Cocktail Party, T. S. Eliot
From Ritual to Romance, Jessie Weston
Peer Gynt, Henrik Ibsen
The Silent Path, M. J. Eastcott
Colour Psychology and Colour Therapy, Deutsch
Radiant Symphony, D. H. Andrews
Parsifal and *Der Ring des Nibelungen*, Richard Wagner
Francis Bacon: From Magic to Science, Paolo Rossi

The Morning of the Magicians, Louis Pauwels and Jacques Bergier

A Treatise on Cosmic Fire, *A Treatise on White Magic*, *The Destiny of the Nations*, *A Treatise on the Seven Rays*, Vol. 2, *Discipleship in the New Age*, Vol. 1, A. A. Bailey

The Woman Who could not Die, Yulia de Beausabre

The Thunder of Silence, J. S. Goldsmith

Symbols of Transformation, C. C. Jung

The Bluebird, Maurice Maeterlinck

The Outsider, *The Mind Parasites*, *An Outline of the New Existentialism*, Colin Wilson

Juno and the Paycock, Sean O'Casey

The Ultimate Revolution, Walter Starcke

Utopia, Thomas More

The New Atlantis, Francis Bacon

The Upanishads

St. John, *St. Luke*, *St. Paul*

The Lord of the Rings, J. R. R. Tolkien

Dune, Frank Herbert

Teach Yourself 'Psychical Research', Raynor Johnson

Battle for the Mind, W. Sargent

The Hidden Persuaders, Vance Packard

The Mystical Ladder, John R. Sinclair